INDEX

ON CENSORSHIP

INDEX ON CENSORSHIP 2 1998

INDEX
ON CENSORSHIP

Volume 27 No 2 March/April 1998 Issue 181

WEBSITE NEWS UPDATED EVERY TWO WEEKS

www.indexoncensorship.org

contact@indexoncensorship.org

tel: 0171-278 2313

fax: 0171-278 1878

Index on Censorship (ISSN 0306-4220) is published bi-monthly by a non-profit-making company: Writers & Scholars International Ltd, Lancaster House, 33 Islington High Street, London N1 9LH. *Index on Censorship* is associated with Writers & Scholars Educational Trust, registered charity number 325003
Periodicals postage: (US subscribers only) paid at Newark, New Jersey. Postmaster: send US address changes to *Index on Censorship* c/o Mercury Airfreight Int/ Ltd Inc, 2323 Randolph Avenue, Avenel, NJ 07001, USA
© This selection Writers & Scholars International Ltd, London 1997
© Contributors to this issue, except where otherwise indicated

Index on Censorship and Writers & Scholars Educational Trust depend on donations to guarantee their independence and to fund research. The Trustees and Directors would like to thank all those whose donations support Index and WSET, including

Scottish Media Group plc
United News and Media
EJB Rose Charitable Trust
Alan & Babette Sainsbury Charitable Fund
Pearson plc Charitable Trust

Former Editors: Michael Scammell (1972-81); Hugh Lunghi (1981-83); George Theiner (1983-88); Sally Laird (1988-89); Andrew Graham-Yooll (1989-93)

EDITORIAL

Out of the darkness

There is no group in the world more censored by the sin of omission than widows. They are absent in the statistics, their daily lives are never described, and they're rarely mentioned in reports on poverty, development or human rights. All too often they fall through the net of humanitarian aid and are neglected by women's movements. Apart from Margaret Owen's pioneering work, *A World of Widows*, we encountered again and again a serious lack of information on the subject.

Widowhood is made more wretched in many traditional cultures by local practices at best archaic and at worst barbaric. But if the lives of widows are hard, those of war widows are particularly so. Sometimes only in their teens and twenties, traumatised by what they have witnessed of torture and killing, often living as refugees (80 per cent of the world's 50 million refugees are women and children), they are treated as the inconvenient detritus of war.

But they are fighting back, as our report demonstrates; women from Srebenica demanding to know where their husbands are buried, Italian widows turning state witness against mafia murderers, Palestinian and Israeli widows determined to participate fully in their societies. These women are tough – and they need to be.

None more so than the widows of Tajikistan, where civil war has left at least 50,000 dead. Their testimonies in our Central Asia file tell of almost intolerable economic hardship and cruel marginalising in a highly patriarchal society. But then the people of Central Asia, a region of great natural beauty and complex social structures, have, like those in the Caucasus (see *Index* 4/97), been marginalised in the fierce struggle for oil supremacy conducted by Russia, China and the USA. Social accountability is not high on the agenda of oil-hungry governments.

★ ★ ★

If the USA had bombed Iraq in February it would have been a war without clear purpose. It was a pretty compromised peace, a deal made with an evil man – but at least the voice of the UN as peacemaker triumphed for the first time in years. If there is one thing to be learned from this dismal situation, it is that the double standards practised by the international community must end: Israel as much as Iraq must be made to comply with UN resolutions if there is to be an end to the mess in Israel/Palestine and stability and justice in the Middle East. ❑

contents

● **Going gone**: Highly-prized editor Stuart Proffitt parted company with publisher Harper Collins in February after it dumped the memoirs of Chris Patten, the UK's last governor in Hong Kong, on owner Rupert Murdoch's instructions. 'RKM has outlined to me the negative aspects of publication, which I fully understand', Eddie Bell, boss of the British arm of the company, wrote in an internal memo. Patten's book is widely expected to shed more light on the handover negotiations, and threatens Murdoch's extensive broadcasting interests in China. Patten has called the move a 'seedy betrayal'.

● **High anxieties** Officials at the World Health Organisation (WHO) have suppressed a scientific analysis which confirms what users have known for years: cannabis is safer than alcohol or tobacco. WHO's first report on the drug in 15 years should have been published in December but, according to one member of the panel that wrote it, officials at the US National Institute of Drug Abuse and the UN Drug Control Programme brought pressure to bear until WHO caved in.

● **It's not – and you can't** In early February, the London *Independent*'s media correspondent Paul McCann devoted two heart-warming columns to the case of 'N', a German artist who uses the vacant advertising slots in underground trains to display drawings of people dancing, drinking and having sex. Everyone liked them, apart from the British Transport Police which confiscated 2,000 drawings, his computer and screen-printing equipment after a raid on N's studio.

● **Not relevant** Another artist, the poet 'Lord Byro', who took his Tax on Sleaze manifesto to the infamous Tatton constituency in the UK's May election, met with a very similar result when he tried to do a Monica Lewinsky and post a St Valentine's poem to Bill Clinton in the *Independent*'s classified section. Deposit returned – and a note saying 'not relevant to the classified Valentines'.

● **Translation chip** Silicon Valley billionaire Ron Unz is using his personal fortune to finance an 'English For Children' initiative, which would ban bilingual education programmes that reach the 3.2 million US children not fluent in the dominant language. A ballot on the initiative is due on 8 June in California.

● **Reconciliation in Colombo** Sri Lankan Catholic officials announced on 16 January that Rome had rescinded the excommunication of Father Tissa Balasuriya (*Index* 2/1997, 5/1997) for his 1990 book *Mary and Human Liberation*.

● **Wheels of chance** Turkey's 79 casinos closed their doors for the last time on 12 February after a government report exposed their alleged links with the local Mafia. 'The casinos lost their original purpose as places to play games of chance and became centres of seduction,' said a spokesman.

● **Flight from Mecca** Meanwhile, 1,000 miles away in lacklustre Luton, the Mecca leisure organisation has been forced to remove its name from a bingo hall after protests from the city's 20,000–strong Muslim community that the company had associated their holy city with gambling.

● **Dead cut(e)** The January issue of *Colors*, a magazine closely affiliated with the Benetton fashion empire, had distribution difficulties in the UK and Japan because of its 'controversial/offensive photos and editorial pieces'. Entitled 'Death: A User's Guide', the issue explores life's ultimate low from a range of quirky perspectives. The UK's largest distributor refuses to stock the issue without a warning on the cover, while Japan's very own Benetton Group has demanded that a guide to vital signs, featuring a naked stiff, should have its loins covered. *Colors* is currently being sued for publishing in an earlier issue the cover of *Final Exit*, a guide to suicide banned in France. Editorial director Oliviero Toscani is due in court in June to answer the charges.

● **Minaret adjustment** In Uzbekistan, the authorities are striving to extinguish an upsurge in religious fervour. Last December, a police chief and several constables were killed in an attack in Namangan, allegedly by members of the Saudi Wahabi sect who, Uzbeks say, were trained in eastern Tajikistan and the Osh region of Kyrgyzstan with Saudi support. At home, the authorities signalled their concern by banning the use of loudspeakers to broadcast the *muezzin*'s traditional call to prayer.

● **Totally unprepared** California's Supreme Court will decide in March whether twin brothers Michael and William Randall, 16, will be allowed to qualify for the Boy Scouts' highest honour, the Eagle Scout badge. The Randalls were expelled from Pack 519 in 1991 because they refused to recite the Cub Scout Promise to 'do my duty to God and my country'. Having won earlier rounds in court, the Randalls have continued scouting, but are now being threatened with exclusion again. The court is also hearing the cases of 12-year-old Katrina Yeaw, who wishes to join the Scouts to learn outdoor skills with her twin brother Daniel, and of Timothy Curran, a Scout master expelled from his post because he is gay.

● **Hands off** A series of AIDS-awareness posters was yanked in January from the hoardings of Budapest after they were condemned by the Self-Regulatory Advertising Board (ORT) for being 'harmful to society'. One displayed a condom-covered index finger pointing towards a mouth; another a hand making an obscene gesture at the letters A-I-D-S. Lambda, which designed the posters, was told by the ORT that 'the self-ended use of eroticism and sexuality, not necessitated by the subject of the advertisement, is forbidden.' ORT recently gave the thumbs-up to a *Cosmopolitan* ad showing a nude female with two male hands cupping her breasts from behind.

● **Clean up** Long-haired musicians have become the latest casualties of balding Prime Minister Nawaz Sharif's mission to give Pakistan's state-owned PTV and the popular FM100 radio a clean bill of moral health. First to go were women models from soap, shampoo and detergent commercials. Next it was the turn of rock-based groups such as Vital Signs, Awaz and Sajjad Ali, whose hit *Babia* is a remake of banned Algerian *rai* singer Cheb Khaled's *Didi*. Deprived of exposure on PTV and FM100, local stars have now defected to Indian satellite channels where they are accessible only to those Pakistanis rich enough to own satellite dishes.

● **Shades of Orson** Paraguay's sober-suited media authority Conatel rescinded its 2 February closure order against Asunción's *Radio Uno* after President Juan Carlos Wasmosy mastered his nerve and stood up, surprisingly, for black humour. *Radio Uno* had broadcast a programme, produced by journalist Juan Pastoriza, which dramatised all too convincingly a coup d'état in progress. One segment featured the mobilisation of troops in anticipation of a presidential order freeing General Lino Oviedo, the former army boss who is currently detained for staging an unsuccessful coup in April 1997. Pastoriza failed to tell listeners that the sequence was, in fact, a comedy. A large part of a panicked Asuncion didn't get the joke.

● **Hello Dolly** The deposed Shah returned to Iranian TV on 1 February, his first appearance since 1979 when the Peacock Throne was overturned by followers of Ayatollah Ruhollah Khomenei. To mark the nineteenth anniversary of the Islamic Revolution, Mohammad-Reza Pahlavi has been allowed back into the limelight as a puppet in a local version of the BBC's highly successful *Spitting Image* programme. Pahlavi is depicted as hopelessly removed from the reality of the mass demonstrations outside the palace, while former Prime Minister Shahpur Bakhtiar is cast as an opium addict and General Azhari, Teheran's former military governor, as a buffoon.

● **Shut up and eat** Food is again at the forefront of the battle for free speech, this time in Texas where talk-show hostess Oprah Winfrey successfully defended herself, her producers and rancher-turned-vegetarian Howard Lyman against Paul Engler, the rancher suing her for US$12 million in damages. Two years ago, Lyman explained on the *Oprah Winfrey Show* how the practice of feeding 'downers', or ground-up cattle, to livestock threatened to taint the US beef industry with BSE, or 'mad cow' disease. Oprah retorted that Lyman's statement had 'stopped her cold' from eating another hamburger. Engler, who has been associated throughout his career with IBP, a long-time supplier of beef to McDonald's, claimed her comment was responsible for a 10-year low in the price of US beef; market analysts attribute it to the collapse of SE Asian demand.
Andrew Elkin

● **The razor's edge** Three years too late for Naglaa Fathy, Egypt's courts finally ruled that the government can ban female genital mutilation (FGM). Fathy was the 14-year-old shown on CNN as a barber sliced off her clitoris with a razor and her father looked on. When the footage was aired during the 1994 International Conference on Population and Development in Cairo, an embarrassed Egyptian government vowed to ban FGM.
Since 1994, the deaths of several girls after circumcision have helped maintain the pressure for a ban. In July 1996, the health minister forbade the practice in government-run clinics and hospitals but the measure was put on hold while opponents mounted a legal challenge. The result was a lower court ruling in June 1997 that only parliament could ban FGM, a ruling that was finally overturned by the Higher State Council on 27 December.
The focus of women's rights activists has now shifted to preventing FGM in practise. 'We still have a big battle in front of us, but the ruling is helpful,' Marie Assaad, co-ordinator of the Task Force on FGM, told reporters. 'I'm working with field workers. Now I can say to them that this is not something imported from the USA or the foreign press. An Egyptian judge thinks it's wrong.'
Eradicating FGM will require considerable government resolve. When surveyed by the government, most women opposed to circumcision thought parental education was the best way to stop it while a parallel programme to educate healthcare workers has also been advocated. The one measure apparently ruled out by popular sensibilities is a programme of sex education in schools.

Meanwhile, the legal battle is not yet fully won. The conservative *shaikh* Yusuf al-Badri, who has mounted a legal challenge, told reporters: 'The judge is human; he can make mistakes.' Badri is challenging the education minister's decision to portray FGM in school textbooks as a physically and psychologically damaging practise. And a suit is still working through the courts against CNN and an Egyptian woman interviewed in the 1994 programme, alleging that they had both defamed Egypt in the eyes of the world.
Rupert Clayton

● *Jambo* to the Fifth Horseman Kenya has become a disaster zone of biblical dimensions. Flood, famine, pestilence and death... it's all there in the latest brochure. The mid-February killing of a British tourist in the deluxe cradle of Kenya's biggest dollar-earning industry was the *coup de grâce*, a knife-thrust into the public image of a nation once held up with little regard for topography as the 'Switzerland' of Africa.

Media coverage of the murder thrust Kenya's problems briefly into the spotlight, but did little to bring home the breadth of the current emergency. Ethnic and political violence in the Rift Valley has caused over than 100 deaths, while disease and starvation have killed far higher numbers in the north east

where *El Niño* – the Fifth Horseman – has caused epic flooding since November, leading to epidemics of such water-borne diseases as cholera, resistant strains of malaria and the 'mysterious' Rift Valley Fever (RVF).

RVF has killed thousands of livestock in Garissa and Wajir and may have hurdled the species barrier to claim an estimated 470 people in the north east. It's hard to tell. The symptoms are alarmingly similar to Ebola virus – high fever and death through haemorrhaging – the very mention of which can empty an African village within seconds. But it is also concentrated in a region decimated by an alleged government-sponsored campaign of ethnic cleansing.

So, in the fatalistic speech codes of both Kikuyu peasant and the official information machine, RVF has evolved into a non-specific fatal complaint often contracted by enemies of the state. More specific, but no less sombre, a new strain of highland malaria killed at least 1,500 people over a period of just two weeks in February and continues to spread unabated.
Lucy Hillier

MICHAEL FOLEY

Role reversal

**The European Convention on Human Rights says freedom of
expression is the rule, limitations on it the exception. And these
exceptions must be narrowly interpreted. This is where any
debate on the role of the media must begin**

For a while everything seemed to be going so well in Ireland: the
government had introduced freedom of information legislation, some
members of parliament were even calling for the abolition of, or at least
severe amendments to, the Official Secrets Act. Politicians spoke of
letting in the light on the workings of government, or operating as if
behind a pane of glass. In Britain free speech campaigners looked to
Ireland with envy. Then everything seemed to change.

True, the Freedom of Information Act will come into effect next
May, but it does not now seem to promise quite as much as when first
mooted a few years ago. We have copper fastened cabinet confidentiality
in a referendum that was so confusing few had a clue what they were
voting for. The number of politicians now calling for the end of the
Official Secrets Act are scarce indeed.

Now it is the British government that is committed to a Freedom of
Information Act. More significantly, perhaps, it is committed to
incorporating the European Convention on Human Rights into British
law. When that takes place, possibly later this year, Ireland will be the
only EU member that has not made the convention part of its domestic
law.

The co-chairman of the Irish Council for Civil Liberties, Michael
Farrell, wrote of the 'embarrassing situation where Ireland is out of step
with all of its European partners'; a situation he said that has not come
about through inadvertence or because Ireland had neglected the issue,
but because the Irish government, according to the Taoiseach (Prime
Minister), Bertie Ahern, had no intention of incorporating the

Convention into Irish law.

It is little wonder that the Taoiseach has no intention of bringing the European convention into Irish law. Successive governments have been unwilling to deal with a whole range of issues relating to a free press and freedom of expression. They have failed to legislate on journalists' rights to protect their sources, promised following the unsuccessful attempt to try ITV's World In Action journalist, Susan O'Keeffe, for refusing to name sources to judicial Tribunal, or on the Defamation Laws, which the Law Reform Commission has recommended be reformed.

If the Convention were to be brought into Irish law, it would bring with it rulings and decisions relating to free expression based on Article 10 of the Convention, which states: 'Everyone has the right to freedom of expression. This right shall include freedom to hold opinions and to receive and impart information and ideas without interference by public authority and regardless of frontiers.'

When the European Court of Human Rights rules that a person's rights under the Convention have been flouted, the country against which the action has been taken has to change its laws. That ruling has effect in every country that has included the Convention in its own body of law.

In implementing the European Convention of Human Rights, the European Court of Human Rights is involved in a delicate balance between individual rights, the rights of the state, the rights of freedom of expression and the right to privacy; the latter is protected under Article 8.

However, it first and foremost recognises the role and function of the media in a modern democracy. In a 1995 judgement, the European Court said: 'Not only does the press have the task of imparting such information and ideas (ie, of public interest), the public also has a right to receive them. Were it otherwise, the press would be unable to play its vital role of public watchdog.'

The Court has ruled favourably in terms of press freedom on a number of important issues, by giving protection to journalists who have refused to divulge anonymous sources, giving journalists access to 'discovered' documents in court cases and by ruling that a high libel award granted by a British court was an infringement of the right to freedom of expression.

Writing in *Freedom, the Individual and the Law*, the English civil liberties lawyer Geoffrey Robertson says the decisions taken at Strasbourg are always cautious and conservative. 'The convention embodies basic rather than progressive standards, which are interpreted so that they may be applied in practice to countries far less economically and socially advanced than the UK.' The Court, for instance, did not rule in favour of the journalists and broadcasters who challenged the Irish government's broadcasting ban in 1991, possibly the only case where it actually ruled in favour of censorship.

Ireland is a signatory of the Convention, and the rulings of the European Court of Human Rights will continue to influence our courts. When Barry O'Kelly of the *Star* refused to name his sources during a civil trial in the circuit court, counsel for the Attorney General admitted the law in this area had developed since a broadcast journalist, Kevin O'Kelly, was imprisoned in the early 1970s for refusing to confirm that a voice on a radio programme was that of the chief of staff of the IRA. Legally, the only difference was a ruling by the European Court in a case won by a British journalist, Bill Goodwin, in 1995 and an indication by his lawyer that O'Kelly's case would be brought to Europe if the judge tried to send him to prison for refusing to name his sources. ❏

Michael Foley is the media correspondent of the Irish Times

JOHN O'FARRELL

Even bastards deserve justice

Freedom of speech is a relative concept in Northern Ireland. Statements made by public figures have to be filtered through the knowledge that every nuance will be examined for fault by opponents and supporters alike. 'Fault' being anything vaguely threatening to the 'other side', or indicative of a 'sell out' for 'our' cause.

To understand what Sinn Fein leader Gerry Adams or the Ulster Unionist's David Trimble mean in their public utterances, the journalist whose job it is to translate their words for public consumption must take into account the internal politics of republicanism or unionism. Both Adams and Trimble, and all other political figures in the North, primarily speak to their own constituencies, leaving those outside the laager perplexed or frightened. Words said to reassure one audience are used by another as evidence of opponent's unreasonableness.

This is politics played as a zero-sum game, where a slight to one is a victory to the other, where even memory is segregated communally. In a land where every betrayal is the final betrayal and every sell-out is total, where 'conciliator' is an insult, what room is there within the 'sides' for freedom of speech? Is there room in the claustrophobic atmospheres of unionism/loyalism or nationaliam/republicanism to challenge the shibboleths designed to trip up the unwary outsider, to unmask the enemy within, to bolster the Big Men who write the rules? And when the rules are rewritten, as happened with the 1994 ceasefires, what happens to those men who cannot change? What happened to Billy Wright?

Billy Wright was 37 when he was assassinated in the Maze,

supposedly the most secure prison in Europe. It holds 700 high-security prisoners, members of the Irish Republican Army (IRA), Irish National Liberation Army (INLA), Ulster Volunteer Force (UVF) and Ulster Defence Association (UDA), most serving long sentences for 'terrorist' activities. The inmates, who consider themselves 'political prisoners' or 'prisoners of war' are segregated into seven fortified compounds, known as H-Blocks.

Wright was the leader of the Loyalist Volunteer Force (LVF), a breakaway faction of loyalists opposed to the ceasefires operated by the UVF and UDA since 1994. When he was imprisoned for eight years last spring, he demanded, and got,

Credit: Rex/Crispin Rodwell

his own wing within the prison, where he was joined by 30 other dissident loyalists. Because of the small size of the LVF contingent, Wright and his colleagues were placed in C and D wings of H6, where a central control unit separated them from wings A and B which housed the incarcerated members of another small dissident faction, this time republican, the INLA.

How did Wright finish up this way? As leader of the Mid-Ulster Brigade of the UVF, he was known and feared as 'King Rat'. From his base in Portadown, he planned, and occasionally carried out, some of the worst atrocities of the entire troubles. His victims included IRA men, and others whom he defined as 'republicans', including two pensioners in an isolated farmhouse, and three teenagers in a mobile shop. He is said to have been involved in the massacre of six catholics watching the Republic of Ireland beat Italy during the 1994 World Cup in an isolated pub in Loughlinisland, County Down.

Wright operated mainly in north Armagh, an area renowned for sectarian tension for three centuries. In 1641, an insurrection by 'some evil-affected Irish papists' included massacres of protestants at Portadown and Blackwatertown. After a sectarian skirmish in 1795 known as 'The Battle of the Diamond', the Orange Order was founded as a unifying protestant force against catholicism. Sectarian bands of brigands, from the 'Peep O'Day Boys', to the 'Defenders' and the 'Ribbonmen' fought it out regularly.

As Belfast industrialised in the nineteenth century, catholic and protestant peasants moved to Belfast seeking work in the shipyards and linen mills. Historians such as Jonathon Bardon claim that relations between the two faiths were good in the city, until Armagh's communal virus arrived with its cheap labour. Long before Billy Wright first picked up a gun as a teenager in 1976, the rural hamlets and grim housing estates between Banbridge, Lurgan and Armagh City were known as the 'murder triangle'. Wright claimed that he was driven to violent defence of his people by the 1976 Kingmills massacre, when the 'Republican Reaction Force' stopped a workmen's bus, separated catholics from protestants, ordered the former back onto the bus and executed all 10 of the latter. This Nazi-style attack was 'justified' by its instigators, the South Armagh Brigade of the IRA, as 'retaliation' for five catholics killed the previous day by loyalists.

Apart from a brief spell in prison soon after he joined the UVF,

Wright was able to evade capture. Royal Ulster Constabulary (RUC) Special Branch officers recall his incredible discipline and focused calmness as he withstood interrogation for up to seven days at a time, answering questions with biblical quotations. At least six attempts were made on his life by the IRA and INLA. His nickname, 'King Rat' struck fear into catholics for 100 miles around Portadown. Then he got a taste for the press.

From the early 1990s, at a period when loyalists were killing more people than the IRA, Wright began briefing journalists on UVF strategy. He believed that by killing IRA members, their supporters or any catholic at all, the IRA would be pressured into calling a ceasefire. Although he claimed that the loyalist ceasefire of October 1994 'was the happiest day of my life', he was soon briefing the press about his unhappiness with the Belfast leadership of the Progressive Unionist Party (PUP), the UVF's mouthpiece.

The PUP's socialist rhetoric was anathema to his fundamentalist protestant beliefs. Wright's ethnic world view, where all catholics were republicans or republican supporters, therefore enemies of Ulster, and therefore targets, was increasingly at loggerheads with the UVF's 'political advisors', who saw common cause with working class catholics, and even lobbied with Sinn Féin leaders on prisoners' issues.

Wright fell back upon the bulwarks of irredentist protestantism and uncompromising loyalism, the Orange Order and the Democratic Unionist Party (DUP). Wright believed the DUP's whispering campaign against the PUP's leaders as agents of MI5. He finally achieved national attention during the 1996 Drumcree protestant marching crisis. On his orders, a taxi driver, Michael McGoldrick, was shot dead, as a warning to north Aramgh catholics. He put pressure on the Portadown Orangemen not to compromise over their 'traditional marching route' down the catholic Garvaghy Road. He also met the Ulster Unionist leader, David Trimble, during the 'siege'. After the crisis, PUP leader Billy Hutchinson went to Portadown to try to get Wright back 'onside', but he was threatened by Wright and his men. The UVF responded by ordering the Mid-Ulster Brigade to 'stand down' and Wright to leave Northern Ireland for good or 'face the consequences'.

Wright responded by organising a rally in support of his 'freedom of speech', which was attended by 2,000 supporters and addressed by Wright and the then MP for Mid-Ulster, the Reverend William

McCrea. 'Boxcar Willie', as the Gospel singing, holy-rollin', true blue
DUP MP was known among his unfortunate catholic constituents,
claims that he condemns all violence. He was just supporting Wright's
freedom of speech. It is also coincidental that McCrea's analysis of the
peace process is identical to Wright's.

The UVF had a simple attitude to his freedom of speech; they
referred to him as 'Billy Wrong', but the clear support among
Portadown loyalists for Wright, and the probability that the PUP would
be ejected from the peace process, meant that the UVF never acted on
their threat. Then the police stepped in. After Drumcree 96, the biggest
fear on the horizon was Drumcree 97. The RUC made it clear that
Wright was the biggest single threat to peace in Northern Ireland,
notwithstanding the resumed IRA campaign. They were desperate to
get him off the streets. In March last year they succeeded. Wright was
convicted and sentenced to eight years for 'threatening a witness'. He
had allegedly told a woman whose son had been beaten by Wright's
'community militia' that if she or her son spoke to the RUC, Wright
would 'fucking shoot him'. The woman is now living under police
protection somewhere in England.

Now let us look at the case. The sole witness, the woman verbally
threatened, has a criminal record for theft and possession of stolen goods.
Wright received the maximum sentence the court could hand down.
Before being removed from the court, Wright argued that 'this (was)
internment for loyalists.' Incarcerated, with fresh martyr status, Wright
attracted to 'his' wing, convicted loyalists unhappy with the peace
process, such as Torrens Knight, responsible for seven catholic deaths in
the Greysteel massacre in 1993 and allegedly directing Loyalist Volunteer
Force (LVF) operations via mobile phone from inside the Maze.

On the morning of his death, a prison officer was removed from the
watchtower overlooking H6, thus missing the two armed INLA men
who climbed over the roof of the Block, cut a hole in a perimeter fence,
approached the van in which Wright and four other LVF prisoners
were about to leave for the visitors compound, and shot Wright five
times in the back, before escaping back to the INLA wings of H6.

No doubt the inquiry into the killing of Billy Wright will try to find
the answers to the many questions raised by this extraordinary set of
circumstances. There is also no doubt that Wright has attained full
martyr status among the thousands who attended his funeral, the

hundreds who have since joined the LVF, and has become a *cause célèbre* for unionist 'constitutional' politicians who will use his demise as a big stick to beat the government and the peace process.

As martyrs for free expression go, Billy Wright is an unlikely candidate. His unswerving beliefs are, however, mirrored in the views of many within the unionist community. Wright pointed up one of the main blocks to real communication, let alone trust, between nationalists and unionists. That is, the belief among Ulster protestants that they are ethnically different from the catholic minority in the province and the majority on the island. If it can be hypothesised that nationalists believe that the roots of the conflict are political and historical, while unionists believe that ethnicity is the root of the problem, then real talks, and meaningful solutions are a long way off. ❑

John O' Farrell, a native of Dublin, has been the editor of Fortnight *magazine in Belfast since 1995*

ISABEL HILTON

The Old Man and the See

The Pope went to Cuba and met the renegade Jesuit. It was not a one-way street and both men gave as good as they got. The Papal visit will change nothing, says Fidel, but Cuba is crumbling and something has to give

'Fidel's chief characteristic,' said Oviedo, pouring a substantial glass of rum, 'is that he fails.' It was an odd remark to make about the man who has led Cuba for more than 35 years, whose regime has withstood the collapse of the Soviet Union and the consequent Cuban economic catastrophe, and who has himself survived all the attempts by the USA to finish him and his Revolution. As failures go, it has great qualities of endurance. But Oviedo had something more subtle in mind. Fidel's revolutionary uprising triumphed in 1959, but Fidel's military part in it reads like a manual of what not to do. One of the Revolution's most celebrated incidents, for instance, the assault on the Moncada barracks in July 1953, was a disaster that cost the lives of most of the men he led and nearly left Fidel languishing in a Batista jail. It was an heroic failure, but a failure nevertheless. Had it not been for the military acumen of others, among them Che Guevara, and the USA's reluctance to give military backing to the rotting Batista regime, history might have turned out differently.

'It's the repeated failure,' Oviedo continued, 'that led him to promote the cult of sacrifice as the essence of the Revolution. It's all very Jesuit.'

I thought of Oviedo's remarks as I listened to Fidel's speech of welcome to the Pope at Havana airport. It was a visit that had inspired a number of expectations and, even when it was over, it was not clear

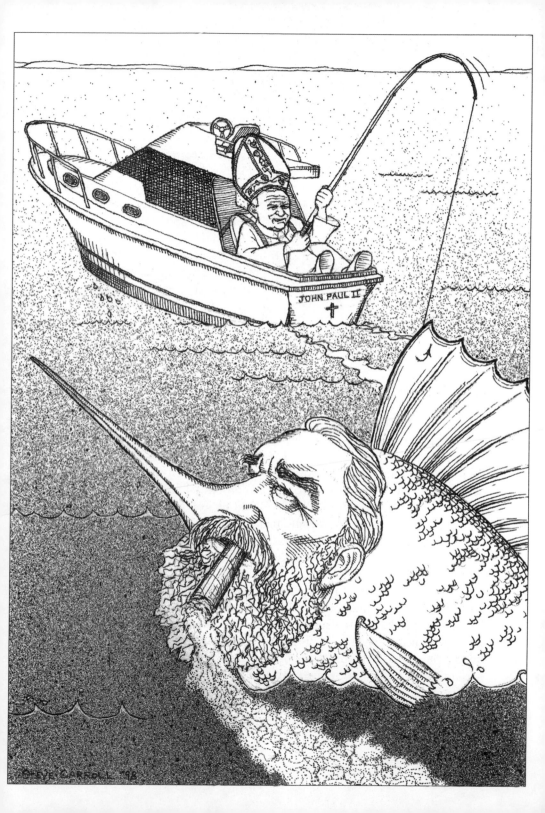

which would be fulfilled. For the anti-Castro camp, the arrival of the Pope evoked memories of Poland in the 1980s, when the Pontiff's appearance as the anti-communist angel confirmed that the end of the regime was nigh. But Cuba, as Fidel was at pains to point out, was not Poland. In Poland, he laboriously explained, to the surprise of those unaccustomed to Fidel's frequent historical revisions, the socialist regime was imposed by force by the Soviet Union – that same Soviet Union on which Fidel had lavished such unstinting praise for so many years. Cuba, though, was another matter.

Fidel had gone to some lengths to recover a measure of control of an event that was a mixed blessing for his regime. After weeks of official media silence, Fidel himself took to the television screen one evening to explain the Pope's visit. His speech turned into a six-hour nocturnal marathon, the headline of which was that the Pope was coming to Cuba as an anti-capitalist, not an anti-communist, and everyone, believer and non-believer alike, was to turn out to welcome him. In Poland, the crowds that turned out to greet the Pope were counted as anti-regime. In Cuba, Fidel had called them out – and could claim them as his own. The parallels between Poland and Cuba were, in any event, too loose to be useful. The relationship between the Pope and Fidel is more subtle than that between the Pope and the communist leaders of his homeland. The Pope may dislike Fidel's socialist politics and mistrust his Jesuit upbringing, but it was not entirely fanciful of Fidel to claim a certain anti-US kinship. The Pope is no more keen on global capitalism and economic sanctions than Fidel. If he could be induced to say so on Cuban soil, then both men would gain something.

At the airport, in a speech that the Pope's entourage later described as an 'ambush', Fidel put his socialist dignity on display and demonstrated to his watchful followers in the Party that the arrival of John Paul II did not spell capitulation to a Church legendary in Cuba for its reactionary politics. His attachment to the cult of sacrifice – the side of him Oviedo would read as the Jesuit – was invoked in full. The speech was a long recitation of the cruelties of history, a justification for Fidel's protean world view and a representation of Cuba as a land soaked in blood. Colonialism, he said, took the lives of millions, the war of liberation against Spain thousands more; now there was a US attempt at genocide that was crushing Cuba.

The Catholic Church, as every Cuban knows was closely aligned with the Spanish regime. And as to the modern day – Fidel invoked his own education at a Jesuit school. 'I asked one of my teachers,' he said, 'why there were no black children in the school. I hope the day will come when no child asks that question in any Catholic school in the world.'

The Pope is not a man easily abashed and, in the days that followed, he gave as good as he got. Fidel says nothing will change as a result of the visit, but the truth is that Cuba has changed already and further change seems unstoppable, despite the Party's continued attachment to its economic dogma. The question posed by Oviedo's description is whether Fidel, even at this late stage in his career, could let go his love of sacrifice enough to allow his people to respond with energy and imagination to the reverses the Revolution has suffered. If he cannot, the final sacrifice could be worse than any that went before.

For now, though, it is not blood that comes to mind in Havana, but mould. The suffocating decay of this once magnificent city, rotting visibly, day after day. Its crumbling facades, potholed streets, sagging balconies and decaying facilities make it look like a city that has just come through a war. There is a war, of sorts, though now it tends not to involve bullets. This is an ideological war, fought out with economic weapons. Like most wars, it is not a simple two-sided affair.

On one hand, there is the USA, with its ossified policy of economic embargo. On the other is Fidel, with his equally desiccated dream of a planned economy. Caught between these two ideological absolutes, a people that is now too busy trying to survive to have time or energy to judge the past or predict the future.

Oviedo is an example: he used to be a state-employed art expert. His last job for the government was to try to develop an international market for Cuban art, currently caught between state regulations that prohibit the private sale of works of art and the urgent need for funds of those who produce it. The result is large-scale illegal export at negligible benefit to Cuba, and large profits to those who resell in New York. Oviedo's conclusion was that in order for Cuban art to have an international market, it first had to have an internal market, an idea that remains heretical in the socialist orthodoxy. He was not exactly fired, but it came swiftly to a parting of the ways. But in a country where everyone is theoretically employed by the state, how does an ex-state employee continue to eat? Oviedo took advantage of one of those unreliable concessions Fidel has been forced to make to allow his people to relieve their hunger: he opened a *paladar*.

'The name comes from a Brazilian soap opera,' he explained. 'The story involved a young woman from the country who ran off to town with her mother's savings and became a successful call girl. The mother pursued her to try to persuade her to return to the provinces – which, of course, the daughter refused to do. The mother then had to make a living. The only thing she could do was cook, so she began in a small way with a tiny restaurant called *Paladar* and, of course, grew rich. The soap opera was tremendously influential,' he laughed. 'A large number of those who watched it took to prostitution. Those who, like me, were unsuitable for prostitution, opened *paladars*.'

These tiny private restaurants are run from the proprietors' houses. The state takes a characteristically ambivalent view: *paladars* are restricted to 12 places and prohibited from selling certain items such as seafood. If a private operator is caught serving lobster, for instance, he risks a heavy fine and the confiscation of all his equipment. Which poses the question, why is it that in almost any *paladar* the main dish on the limited menu is seafood? Lobster is particularly popular. It is not just in the *paladars* that the rules are illusory. A good professional salary in Cuba is now worth the equivalent of 50 cents (US) a day, enough to buy a bottle of milk on the black market. The result is that the function of a professional post – or any lesser-paying job – is not to sustain life but to provide the means of making a living by dealing privately. The factory workers steals the product to sell, the Internet provider undercuts his enterprise by offering connections privately to clients, the TV man will fit up a black-market satellite dish and the bar tender sells bootleg liquor under the counter. It all flourishes unchecked because the policemen, too, rely on the black market – they live on the bribes they collect in return for leaving this mass of commerce alone.

Those whose professional lives do not afford them black market opportunities have begun to desert their posts for jobs that give them direct access to the only currency that is worth anything – the US dollar. The man who is washing up in the tiny kitchen of a *paladar* turns out to be a professor of psychiatry who will sit down and discuss the revisionist view of Freud in perfect English; the bellhop in a tourist hotel has a PhD in physics; the coach driver used to be a doctor. Now he lives on the passengers' tips and the profits to be had from siphoning the fuel from the coach's tank.

But this was not the Cuba that Fidel described to the Pope at the José Marti International Airport. 'In Cuba,' Fidel told the Pope, 'you will find fewer old people without hospital beds, more teachers in the schools than in any country you have visited.' It may once have been true, but the hospitals are out of aspirin and the schools have no books. 'In my daughter's school,' a mother complained to me, 'we discovered that her teacher was asking the children for a share of their packed lunch. Every night, when I go to bed, I ask myself, what are we going to eat tomorrow? We struggle to put together a packed lunch for her, each of us sacrificing something. And the teacher was taking it.'

'Did Fidel realise,' I asked Oviedo, 'that he had parted company from reality?' Oviedo shrugged. 'There is a group that lives in enormous privilege, an inner circle. They have grand houses and telephones that work and plenty to eat,' he said, 'and they are not very bright.' Another friend gave me a cup of coffee in a cup with a broken handle. The cup had been stolen from a ministry canteen. Theft of canteen crockery – along with anything else that is not tied down – by workers desperate either for cups or for something to sell had become such a headache in the ministry that action had to be taken. The solution was an inspired example of absurdist bureaucratic art: the ministry decided that nobody would steal the cups if they had no handles, so, as the replacement cups arrived, a functionary was assigned to break them off. 'People still steal them,' said my friend. 'But it......... does bring their resale value down a bit.'

Cuba has become an absurdist state, full of contradictions that coexist without resolution. The USA maintains the fiction that the world supports its embargo against Cuba and that, sooner or later, the blockade will bring Fidel down. Fidel maintains the fiction that the embargo is the main cause of Cuba's economic troubles and claims that he is fighting to have it lifted. The people maintain the fiction of believing him, except for people like Oviedo. 'It's only the embargo that's keeping Fidel in power,' he said, gloomily pouring another glass of bootleg rum. 'Without the embargo, he would have no excuse. But the great enemy over there is still sufficiently scary. He can say, 'Look, without me, the Americans will come and get you!''

After two more glasses of rum, the theory had become more elaborate. Fidel was not just maintained in power by the embargo, he argued. He had been created by the US military-industrial complex to satisfy that creature's need for an enemy. Their mutual hostility kept the military of both sides to the fore and therefore happy. Behind Oviedo, a parrot in its cage fluffed out its feathers. After one last baleful glare at its master, it swivelled its head round 180 degrees and sunk its beak into its wing weathers. One eye opened, gave a long slow blink and closed, firmly. Oviedo had launched himself into the wide uncharted ocean of conspiracy theory. But, wild as his ideas were, they were no more absurd than the arguments that Washington puts forward for maintaining the embargo against Havana. And in neither capital are more reasonable opinions considered acceptable.

'Fidel blames the embargo for this disaster,' said a travelling companion as we sped along the empty highway that leads, eventually, to Santiago de Cuba. 'But why is there no food? In this country you just have to spit a tomato pip out in the evening and there's a plant the next morning. At the time of the Revolution, there were more Jersey cows in Cuba than people, but Fidel had the idea that we could cross-breed oxen with dairy cattle and get a draught animal that gave milk. So now we have neither. They imported Vietnamese buffaloes and they died. Then they brought Peking ducks, and we were all going to eat duck every day, but they died too. They put up electric fences to keep the cattle in – which is fine when you have electricity. But we don't, so they escaped.' 'I was a teacher at the time of the Revolution,' she said. 'I volunteered to go and teach in the mountains. I cried for a week once I got there. I just wanted to go home. Then I stopped crying and looked at the children. They had nothing, but they were there every day. They had to walk for miles but they always arrived by eight in the morning. I was happy there in the end. Now I don't believe in the Revolution and I don't believe in God either.'

Others have replaced their faith in socialism with its promise of paradise now with the more nebulous but more constant promise of paradise hereafter. All over Cuba, churches of every denomination are filling up. *Santeria*, the religion of the slaves, is thriving, too. It is partly because it is now permitted to proclaim a religious faith, and also because the sanctions that used to apply – the threat of the loss of a job or a hard-won privilege– have lost their bite. Nobody imagines now that the jobs that the state can offer point to a future. For those already in them, this realisation is dismal enough. But for the young, the lack of a future is eating away at the present.

Why not turn to crime when all around people are breaking the law to survive? Why pursue a university career if a professor of psychiatry is washing dishes in a *paladar*? However hard he scrubs, he won't earn as much in a week as the 16-year-old prostitute can make in a day from the sex tourists who have now added Cuba to their own priapic maps of the world. Prostitutes now infest Havana. Their alert, anxious presence in every bar and on every kerbside is only one of many signs of a society stretched to its limits, its facade of socialist sufficiency and egalitarianism cracking in a crazy pattern of unexpected misfortune and undeserved rewards.

Havana 10 years ago was universally drab, its pre-revolutionary colours buried under a thick coating of socialist uniformity, its only quirk the living museum of US cars from the 1950s, kept alive for decades by ingenuity and devotion. But that uniform coating is worn into patches now and Havana is a palimpsest. In parts it is the city that time forgot: a place with few functioning telephones and collapsing public transport, where the car marooned with its bonnet up is as likely to have run out of petrol as to have broken down. In those parts, Havana is a city stranded in an ideology of the 1960s, now too exhausted to keep its own wheels turning. In other places there are islands of consumerism that have already turned the city's revolutionary history into a commodity in which the past and the future are randomly juxtaposed.

The Hotel Coiba in Havana is a showcase of these oddities: built by Spanish investors as a prestige project, it is a brutal vision of the Havana that international capital would create if Cuba's regime were to collapse in disorder. In the spacious cocktail bar, three stately US cars sit, polished and gleaming, testament to Cuba's ingenuity and loneliness turned into a fashion statement. On giant screens black and white movies from the 1950s, in which Cuba appears as a Carmen Miranda fantasy of singing mulattas, the decadence of the Batista years stripped of its political resonance, a backdrop to a dollar bar.

Step out of the bar and similar cars are still being nursed along the potholed streets. Go to Santa Clara, four hours drive from Havana, and public transport depends on even more ancient vehicles – horse-drawn carts that serve as buses in the city centre. Santa Clara is reduced to the age of the horse, even as the advance guard of capitalism peddles 1950s' nostalgia to jaded tourists.

The visit was described as a tussle between opposing ideologies, but it wasn't that simple. One or two of the Pope's prelates permitted themselves a barbed comment or two – like the archbishop of Santiago, Pedro Meurice Estiu, who said too many Cubans 'have confused patriotism with a party'. The Pope, though, declared for religion, morality, liberty and for the necessities of life – a list that few could object to in Cuba. But his most intricate wish was for Cuba to open to the world 'and the world to Cuba'. It was an appeal to Castro to loosen his grip and an appeal to the USA to abandon its obsolete armlock. If both were to heed him, Cuba could quickly rediscover prosperity and a sense of purpose, her young people might return to their books and her professors leave the kitchen sink. Sadly – if, as seems more likely, neither relents – Fidel may get his last and greatest sacrifice. ❏

Isabel Hilton is a writer and broadcaster. She is currently writing a book on the Panchen Lama

THE WHITE ISSUE

I'm Ofay, You're Ofay
A conversation with Noel Ignatiev, Cornel West, and William "Upski" Wimsatt

The Overcoat
Hilton Als on William Burroughs and black fashion

How to Make Love to a White Man
Don Belton on danger, desire, and interracial romance

Africans of European Descent
Michael Chege on the destiny of white Africa

White like Canada
George Elliott Clarke on the politeness of whiteness

Along the Color Bar
Klaus de Albuquerque on growing up colonial

The Mercenary Position
Howard French on white mercenaries and the end of the French empire

Pale Face, Red Neck
Darius James and James Goad on "white trash" and white power

Autobiography of an Ex-White Man
Walter Benn Michaels on why race is not a social construction

Losing It
France Winddance Twine on white mothers of black children

Ethnic Hash
Patricia Williams on race and gastronomy

The Yellow Negro
Joe Wood on Japan, hip hop, and the meaning of blackface

The Shirley Temple of My Familiar
Ann DuCille on whiteness and popular culture

The Feminazi Mystique
bell hooks on Leni Riefenstahl and white feminism

Declaration of Independence
Jamaica Kincaid on the myth of America

Duke University Press, Box 90660, Durham, NC 27708-0660.
To place your journal order using a credit card, call toll-free 888.DUP.JRNL (888.387.5765).
Fax: 919.688.3524, http://www.duke.edu/web/dupress/
Visit the *Transition* Web site: http://web-dubois.fas.harvard.edu/transition/

TRANSITION 73

Widows: life after death

CAROLINE MOOREHEAD

A world of silence

Despite the proliferation of human rights groups and a growing concern with free expression worldwide, no group is as silent and invisible as the world's widows. Widows fall through the cracks of everyone's agenda. They are silent, invisible. The victims of traditional custom and practice in many parts of the world, and the uncounted legacy of war from Europe to Afghanistan

The woman who stares serenely out of the hugely successful advertisement for the UK pension company Scottish Widows has her hair covered modestly and retiringly by what looks like a veil. But under it is a beautiful and confident face, smiling mysteriously, with an expression that suggests seduction rather than grief. If her age is a little ambiguous – 40 perhaps, even 45 – there is nothing ambiguous about how she seems to feel about her future. The money Scottish Widows has paid out to her is clearly going to be spent not on seclusion and mourning but on pleasure.

This advertisement could only appear in the West, and even here, with its overtones of prosperity and sensuality, it sits uneasily with the reality of most widows' lives. In the developing world it would have no meaning at all. There, to be a widow is to endure a life, almost without exception, of neglect, discrimination, harassment, loneliness, ostracism and poverty. In the West, a widow frequently suffers a harsh drop in income and some loss of status when her husband dies, but there is no legal or institutional discrimination against her. In the Third World, she may lose all she has. With the death of a husband, the already sharp divide between a Western woman and one in the developing world widens into a vast gulf. Quite apart from the differences in life expectancy between men and women, cultural norms and taboos, customary and state laws governing inheritance, and most devastatingly, Aids, all combine to make widowhood a time of nightmare. Unlike the smiling Scottish Widow, today's Third World widows are frequently very young, sometimes only in their teens.

What all widows share, wherever they come from, is the fact that there are far more of them than widowers. Almost all married women will find themselves at some moment widowed. In Britain, the 1991 census showed that 43 per cent of women over the age of 65 were widows. In many parts of the developing world, that figure rises to over 70 per cent, though reliable figures are not easy to come by: widows are often missed in censuses, especially when they are elderly and shuffled around between relatives. In Zimbabwe, there are 88 widows for every 12 widowers. Widowers also tend to remarry; after a devastating earthquake in Maharashtra in northern India in 1988, 80 per cent of the men who lost wives remarried within two months.

Yet widows, as a subject in their own right, are curiously neglected, both by the women's movement and by the international humanitarian community. The literature that appears in the West on development, poverty, gender and human rights is almost totally silent on widows; and even where violence against women is examined, the particular form it can take against widows is ignored. A mixture of ignorance about what non-governmental organisations are doing for women in Africa and the Middle East, and reluctance to interfere in what is regarded as a private realm of grief, continues to create a form of censorship by silence. The document agreed by governments at the 1995 Fourth World Conference on Women, the Global Platform for Action, makes no specific mention of them; nor, beyond a commitment to make the 'human rights of women and the girl child.....an inalienable and indivisible part of universal human rights', does the 1994 Vienna Declaration and Programme for Action on Human Rights.

In many parts of the world, the power of men over women's lives remains absolute, and the rights of widows, if they can be called 'rights', are infringed repeatedly, casually and without remorse. As if to confirm their status, widows in Bangladesh and India are often refereed to as *rand*, *randi* or *raki* – words that mean prostitute and whore.

There have been many moving accounts written in the West about the loneliness of widowhood, and the sense of social rejection that follows the death of a husband. But there are, increasingly, networks of self-help groups, under increasingly powerful and vocal organisations of retired and elderly people, to advise on pensions, housing and psychological problems. Just the same, according to the American Association of Retired People (AARP) in Washington, 21 per cent of widowed women (11 million in the USA, compared with 2 million widowed men), live in 'poverty' which they define as under US$6000 a year. European studies show that older people are one of the poorest groups in the European Union today, with older women at the bottom end of the scale.

Even so, once you leave the safe enclave of the developed world, widowhood takes on a far bleaker and more frightening colour. Apart from anything else, it can start extremely young. In many African countries, up to 70 per cent of girls are married by the age of 19. The average age at which a girl marries in India is a little over 14. Though most countries now have laws prohibiting child marriage, the practice of betrothing infants, and sometimes unborn babies, continues, with young brides regarded as more biddable, more likely to bear sons and with their virginity guaranteed. In Iran, the revolutionary leaders have turned back the clock: after the departure of the Shah, laws were introduced to reduce the marriageable age of girls from 18 to 13. It is not unknown nowadays to find women whose lives have been a cycle of repeated widowhood. Margaret Owen, whose book *A World of Widows* (Zed Books, London 1996) looks at the Third World in detail, tells the story of Lakshmi, an elderly Hindu widow in Bangladesh who had been married at 10 and widowed at 12, then forbidden by Hindu law from marrying again. When first widowed she lived with her husband's mother, who had herself been widowed at 14. They were later joined by Lakshmi's widowed mother, and Lakshmi worked as a servant to support the three of them. Since their death she lives alone, keeping alive by begging or searching for grains of rice spilled along the village paths.

Many studies of widowhood carried out in Africa and Asia concern inheritance and the much-debated tradition of levirate, whereby a widowed woman marries her deceased husband's brother. An area in which Western concepts and Third World practices conflict, levirate is variously regarded as essential in ensuring economic support for widows and their children or, in an age of increased awareness of women's rights, barbaric, in that it removes all question of choice from a widow. Stories abound of women who have refused the marriage imposed on them only to find themselves evicted from their homes, their children taken away by the husband's family, their possessions and land seized. Though the practice of *sati* – immolation on a husband's funeral pyre – providing '30,000 years of paradise, as many years as hair on a human body', was made a criminal offence in India over 100 years ago, occasional cases are still reported.

For many widows throughout Asia and Africa the death of a husband spells poverty, instant and crushing. Laws, whether modern, traditional or religious, almost invariably discriminate against them. Once the 'cleansing' rituals surrounding a death have been performed – it can be the shaving of the widow's head to wash away the spirit of the deceased, compulsory sexual relations with a male relation, or a 'de-sexing' process which involves removing all bright colours or jewellery – the process of stripping the home may begin. Unprotected by the law, these widows find themselves rapidly sentenced to slave labour or work in sweatshops, and sometimes reduced to prostitution. Even where the law offers some protection, illiteracy makes the taking over of a husband's small business impossible, while the powerlessness of women makes them particularly vulnerable to greedy relations. Where the tradition of levirate once brought with it a certain security, an obligation on the husband's family to care for his widow, the breakdown in social structures and increasing urbanisation have removed even those safeguards. 'Chasing off' and 'grabbing property' have become such common inheritance disputes that the phrases have entered the vernacular in parts of India and Bangladesh. In Malawi, the practice has become so extreme that law reform proposals refer to the 'rampaging relatives of the deceased'. How, asked a Kenyan lawyer not long ago, 'can a chattel inherit a chattel?'

The children of widows fare little better. Whether kept as servants by their father's family, or removed from school and sent out to work, their future reflects their mother's standing. The girls, in particular, feature prominently among the children working in carpet factories in the Middle East and among street children and child prostitutes.

The war and violence now seemingly endemic throughout parts of Asia, Latin America and Africa have sharply increased the number of widows – and their problems – in recent years. In 1991, Uganda was said to have about 200,000 war widows. Today, over 30,000 widows of the long wars in Afghanistan are reported to be begging on the streets of Kabul, forbidden by the fundamentalist Taliban from working. As if war widowhood were not enough, men in Cambodia, where the Pol Pot years killed or 'disappeared' a disproportionate number of men, are said to resort to far higher levels of domestic violence, since they can replace wives without difficulty.

Over 80 per cent of the world's refugees, now numbered at close on 50 million, are women and children. Abruptly made the head of their households, widowed or separated women find themselves having to take decisions and deal with officials in ways they have had no preparation for. During the flight from their homes they live in constant fear of theft, rape and extortion. Few stories are more terrible then those told by the Somali women who fled the violence of the warlords at home for camps in Kenya. In 1990, a 33-year-old Somali woman called Julia crossed the border into Kenya with her husband. It was dark and they were attacked by bandits on the frontier. Her husband was killed, after having been forced to watch her being gang-raped and her face scarred with knives. Left for dead, Julia was rescued by other refugees and taken to hospital, where she was later found to be both pregnant and HIV positive. She gave birth to the baby, abandoned it in a latrine and committed suicide. Though it would not have covered Julia's fate, after the rape of Muslim women in the former Yugoslavia, rape of women by enemy soldiers was designated under international law as a 'war crime', indictable under the international War Crimes Tribunal.

In Guatemala, where repression and terror have long since been a part of daily life, and where the military dominates, using its power to corrupt and subvert the entire judicial system, there are now said to be 'no political prisoners – just bodies and disappearances'. Most of them are men. 'Disappearances' are terrible for widows. Abduction and interrogation under torture are carried out by security forces and vigilantes, and those who witness the atrocities cannot afford to testify without risking becoming victims themselves. Silence, self-censorship prevails.

Judith Zur spent two years working with war widows in the province of El Quiche in the north-west highlands of Guatemala. La Violencia, as it is known, began in the late 1970s, when the army argued that it had to defend the state against enemy forces and ideas. This really meant the Indian population. The early victims were so-called guerrillas; they soon became all 'potentially dangerous' civilians. Between 1981 and 1983, 15,000 people 'disappeared', most of them men, leaving women too frightened to speak out.

El Quiche was one of the provinces hit hardest by the military. In some villages half the population 'disappeared'. The mutilated bodies that turned up by the roadside were often too disfigured to be identified and the women who came to look were unsure whether their men were among them. Left in limbo, unable to mourn properly, too terrified to give evidence, feeling half-complicitous with the killers, they have found it impossible to make sense of their lives.

To the terror of death was added that of rape. Today, reports Judith Zur, it is hard to find a Mayan girl of over 11 who has not been raped. And 'disappearances' go on, many of the victims being singled out for attack on account of their role as leaders of indigenous movements. Rosa Pu, a young Guatemalan, lost her first husband, who 'disappeared' in 1981. She went to work for CONAVIGUA, an association of widows, to try to trace him. Soon, she was being followed and threatened. She married again, this time the leader of the National Council of Disappeared People of Guatemala, Luis Miguel Solis Pajarito, and had a child. Luis Miguel too has 'disappeared'.

"They thought, that by kidnapping that man,' Rosa Pu wrote in a poem about her missing husband, 'They have won, and have defeated him./ But that's not what happened./ He has won./ He has beaten them? Because he gave himself body and soul to the people./ They thought that by kidnapping that man/ They would silence many/ But that's not what happened/ Now there's more voices that cry out...'

In Europe, one of the most remarkable groups of widows is those who owe their widowhood to the mafia, and who took the extraordinarily brave step of breaking with the tradition of silence and turning state witness against mafia murderers. They have paid for their courage dearly.

In October 1984, a prosperous horse butcher from Palermo in Sicily called Cosimo Quattrocchi was murdered with eight of his employees in what became known as the Piazza Scaffa massacre. He had been doing business with a mafia meat cartel in Catania, who nearly ruined him, and had recently decided to go elsewhere for his meat. His widow, Pietra la Verso, not only defied the mafia and tried to keep the business going but identified her husband's killers, mafiosi meat dealers, to the police. Over the next few months her shop was boycotted and the family ostracised. Her children turned against her. The men she had accused, after a lengthy trial, were all acquitted. To pay her debts she has had to sell everything she owns.

At the trial, Pietra La Verso was the only relative of the eight murdered men to give evidence. She would probably have chosen to remain silent herself, had it not been for the support of a remarkable organisation, born in the early 1980s out of the war between the mafia and the Italian state. The Association of Sicilian Women against the Mafia, begun by Umberto Santino and Anna Puglisi, started life as an offshoot of a small research organisation in Palermo and gathers material on the mafia.

At the end of the 1970s there was a spate of killings of policemen, magistrates and bodyguards by the mafia. Two women, Giovanna Terranova, widow of a highly respected criminal court judge shot by the mafia in 1979, and Rita Costa, widow of an attorney-general who had bravely signed arrest warrants for a number of powerful mafia drug traffickers, took a petition, with over 30,000 signatures, to Rome demanding that existing laws be tightened up. They returned to Palermo and began to contact other widows like themselves.

In the early days, the group welcomed only the widows of those men who had died in the service of the state. But as the war between the mafia and the police became more murderous, the mafia women themselves began to come forward to give evidence. The Association decided to embrace all who had been widowed in Sicily's long-running civil war. Today the widows, many of them like Pietra La Verso impoverished and isolated, meet and help each other during trials and before lawyers. After the particularly brutal summer of 1992, when two prominent judges, Giovanni Falcone and Paolo Borsellino, were murdered together with Falcone's wife and a number of bodyguards, the widows led a public protest against the massacres, coming up with a symbol to express the revulsion of Palermo's citizens towards the mafia.

One morning, they hung white sheets from their balconies above Palermo's streets. Their neighbours, understanding the gesture, did the same, sometimes writing phrases condemning the killers on their sheets. Shops agreed to sell sheets for what they call 'anti-mafia' use at a 30 per cent discount. Soon, the entire city was draped in white. The women who belong to the group refuse to call themselves 'mafia widows'. They say, as Giovanna Terranova puts it, that the label gives them 'a sense of physical violence; as if they had shot us as well'.

Nothing, perhaps, has had a worse impact on widows than Aids. By 1994, according to the World Health Organisation, over 18 million men and women, and one million children, had been infected. By 2000 this figure is estimated to reach 40 million. Aids has created a whole new generation of widows, infected with the HIV virus, giving birth to infected babies, and liable to die far more quickly than the infected men because they are usually malnourished, overworked and very poor. One doctor in Zimbabwe told Margaret Owen that only 1 per cent of widows of men who had died from Aids in his hospital ever returned for check-ups. Widowhood is always terrifying; with Aids it becomes unendurable.

Most of the work done on Aids in the developing world comes from Uganda, one of the countries hardest hit and one of the most open about the illness. In 1994, almost 10 per cent of the population – about 1.5 million people – were HIV positive. Elsewhere in Africa, the taboos and silence surrounding widows have made them especially vulnerable. Since widows are not supposed to form new relationships, they have no access to the health care that might protect them from Aids or unwanted pregnancies. Family Planning Associations in several developing countries have a policy of not seeing widowed or unmarried women. Margaret Owen reports that a member of Kenya's FPA looked astonished when asked whether they provided a service for widows. They did not recognise widows, they told her, as potential candidates.

In societies in which it is often felt that it is the woman's fault if her man gets ill, the growing debilitation of a man dying of Aids is blamed on his wife's lack of care. When he dies, she may be driven from the village. Polygamy, still practised in parts of Africa and the Middle East, adds to the risk of the virus spreading. Older widows, who might normally hope to be cared for in later life by their sons, find themselves looking after orphaned grandchildren and even great grandchildren, some of whom are themselves HIV-positive. Aids has also contributed to the rise in the number of child brides, with men wanting to be certain that there is no chance of marrying an HIV-positive woman. It is not unusual to find women, still in their 20s, already widowed twice through Aids, themselves HIV-positive, bringing up HIV-positive children.

Though terrible, the spread of Aids may help with what Margaret Owen sees as one of the only solutions to the unhappy and impoverished lives of Third World widows. If widows were made economically secure, she argues in her book, then they would be able to control their own futures. She has set up an organisation called Empowering Widows in Development to act as a reference point and provider of information, particularly for researchers working in Third World countries, who have already achieved a certain amount of work in the field, but in which there is as yet little Western interest or involvement.

Something of this need for economic independence has been behind the founding of a number of self-help groups now being set up in parts of Africa and Asia. Like Palermo's Women against the Mafia, there is Uganda's TASO (the Aids Support Organisation of Uganda) founded in 1987 by Noerine Kaleeba, after her husband died from Aids contracted through a blood transfusion. TASO's early members were the wives of men dead or dying from Aids and couples still battling against it. Today it acts as a highly efficient NGO, offering counselling and outpatient care. Of the 16 founders, only Noerine is still alive.

Then there is Kenya's Widows and Orphans Society, set up in 1991 to help what founder Hilda Orimba believes to be half the adult female population of the country: widows struggling to cultivate their land, educate their children and repel the demands of their avaricious relations. In Bangladesh, there is now a project that invites poor widows to become shareholders in a profit-making company farming fish. The widows contribute their labour by digging ponds on land donated by the richer villagers. Elsewhere, organisations support women widowed by wars, like the remarkable AVEGA in Rwanda, the 'Widows of Genocide', set up to help women who lost husbands and children in the genocide and who now find themselves, for the first time in their lives, alone. One of its founders lost 31 members of her family in the killings.

What caught Margaret Owen's attention, as she travelled around the world gathering research data, was the number of women who, freed from despotic marriages, had no intention of marrying again. They told her that they feared for the welfare of their children, were frightened of contracting Aids and did not want to risk losing what little they had been able to put together. Furthermore, few could see any prospect of making a decent marriage. Under the laws and conventions now in force throughout the world, there is no reason why they should not be free to act as they wish – except that breaches of the Women's Convention, like breaches of all UN conventions, carry no sanctions.

But there is a far more important reason why the position of widows

in many parts of the world is so dire: like internal refugees, they slip through the cracks in provision. No-one takes formal and specific responsibility for their welfare – not the development nor health programmes; not the women's movement, not governments, not the Aids projects.

In an age of proliferating NGOs, of international organisations and of a heightened awareness of almost every facet of the human condition, widows are invisible. Perhaps they have no option, as Christina Obbo, an anthropologist who has worked in Kenya and Uganda, puts it, but to become 'wide-eyed, resourceful and tough'. ❏

Caroline Moorehead is a writer on human rights and producer of the BBC programme 'Human Rights, Human Wrongs'.

A WORLD OF WIDOWS
Margaret Owen

Neglected by social policy researchers, international human rights activists and the women's movement, the status of the world's widows - legal, social, cultural and economic - is an urgent issue given the extent and severity of the discrimination against them. This book provides a global overview of the status of widows around the world.

'A fascinating and very detailed book about almost all aspects of the lives, lack of rights and in many cases systematic mistreatment of widows throughout the world ... essential reading for anyone concerned with human rights and development issues.'

Kate Young, WOMANKIND Worldwide

'Margaret Owen succeeds in presenting a tantalizing view of widow's lives and of the complex social rules surrounding widowhood in Africa and Asia.'

Martha Chen, Harvard Institute for International Development

'This is an important book in its plea to reconsider the rights of widows universally ... I would recommend it to all engaged in the struggle for women's empowerment.'

Wendy Harcourt, Development Journal

✂ -

Please send me _____ copies of *A World of Widows* @ £13.95/$19.95 Pb

☐ I enclose a cheque payable to Zed Books Ltd for £ _____

Name _____

Address _____

_____

ZED BOOKS
7 Cynthia Street, London N1 9JF, UK
Tel: (0)171-837 4014 Fax: (0)171-833 3960

MICHAEL GRIFFIN

Hostages

Kabul's war widows have become a bargaining chip in a bid, by the Taliban and relief agencies alike, to deflect attention from the abiding issue of human rights for all Afghan women

'She gives the impression of being cut into bits, set adrift; the limbs seem to lengthen indefinitely...for a long time she commits errors of judgement as to the exact distance to be negotiated.' In 1959, Frantz Fanon described the hallucinatory experiences of women who had removed the veil to penetrate, and carry out bomb attacks in, the French quarters of Algiers and Oran during the Algerian war of independence.

Nearly 40 years on, women in Kabul have run the equation in reverse. Those who had lived unveiled since childhood now find their scope of vision narrowed to a 30° tunnel through a claustrophobic grille, all that is provided for by the *burkha*, a pleated, all-embracing garment, shaped like a shuttlecock, that renders the public identity null.

It distorts distance, muffles hearing and poses the constant hazard of being run down by the fleets of silent cycles that throng the capital. Wearers recognise former friends only from shoes or rings, for they are similarly invisible on their rare excursions from home. As the day lengthens, the temperature soars and breath-marks moisten the light-blue cloth in a facsimile of silenced lips.

Women who trip on the broken streets or lose their footing on the icy pavements of an Afghan winter, face a deeper danger by revealing flesh or underclothing. The penalty for exposing the face was set at 29 lashes by the *Amr Bil Marof Wa Nai Az Munkir* (the Department for the Propagation of Virtue and the Prevention of Vice), a 100-strong 'religious' police force established by the Taliban leader Mullah Mohammed Omar the day his troops captured the capital on 27 September 1996. After 35 years of hippy tourism, US influence and the modernising impact of Soviet occupation, the elusive autonomy of Kabuli women ended overnight.

Tens of thousands of social workers, secretaries, office cleaners and engineers were sent home, paralysing a government in which 25 per cent of the staff were female. The decision affected 7,790 female teachers, the backbone of education, and 8,000 graduates at Kabul University, whose female dormitories had just been rebuilt by ousted President Burhanuddin Rabbani during a hiatus in the city's four-year siege.

For Kabul's 30–50,000 war widows, few of whom could afford the

US$30 *burkha,* the restoration of the Islamic dress code for women amounted to a formal sentence of house arrest and slow starvation. A 1995 survey of 1,100 of them found that one third had borrowed to survive in the previous month; 60 per cent had nothing left to sell; and 13 per cent had been forced into beggary. They – and the quarter of a million children supported by widows in Kabul – lived on green tea and *nan* (bread), with an occasional dish of yoghurt. Without a *burkha,* they could neither shop nor gather water; with one, they were free to collect alms.

Under the Taliban, widows were doubly victimised. Not only were they denied paid employment, they lost access to food aid which had to be collected by male relatives. The possibility that they might have none left was beyond the comprehension of the authorities. Mullah Ghaus, the new foreign minister, was 'astonished' at the resulting level of international concern for 'such a small percentage of the working population.'

After 17 years of war, the UN estimated the number of Afghan widows at around 700,000, a statistic – like most others in this country – that is deeply flawed. Soviet-backed President Mohammed Najibullah had virtually institutionalised the widow by establishing women's councils and development agencies to liaise between them and the social services ministry. Prior to that, she and her offspring would expect to be taken care of by the extended family.

Najibullah's successor, Rabbani, absorbed these mechanisms into the *mujahedin* administration, swelling the lists with the dependants of the victims of the two sieges of Kabul, which had claimed 20-30,000 lives by the middle of 1996. They were taken up enthusiastically by donors and with little scrutiny: indeed the line between the authentic 'widow' and the women who were economically vulnerable, became hopelessly blurred as the siege tightened and food grew scarce.

But with no clearer line of access to females in the more conservative rural areas, projects for widows provided the easiest means for agencies in Afghanistan to nail gender credentials – and the equally-important rubric, 'income-generating schemes' – to their fund-raising mastheads. 'Widows are and remain an emotive issue,' admits Jolyon Leslie, the UN regional coordination officer in Kabul, 'for whom it has been easy to secure support.'

Long before the Taliban, widowhood was the next best criterion –

after wealth – for exemption from the cultural conventions which prevented women from working or moving around unveiled. And in a city in which half the 2 million population lived off relief, Kabuli widows had at least a ticket to eat, and that was a tradeable commodity both in the *bazaar* and an extended family similarly beset by bombardment.

Few agencies, however, had bothered to make their widows' projects credible outside the context of conflict. The bakery and sewing schemes, supported by the World Food Programme (WFP), UNICEF and other specialised UN agencies, did little to instill self-sufficiency or business skills among their largely illiterate beneficiaries. They were paid a 'salary' of relief food, but below-market prices for their bread or quilts, which were distributed elsewhere under the Kabul emergency programme.

The arrival of the Taliban heralded a curious transformation in the widow's already anomalous status. Like all working women in Kabul, she was sent home and denied the right to leave without a *burkha*. Yet the crowds of blue-veiled beggers were a constant rebuttal of the Taliban claim that all Afghan women had the economic support of male family members. She owed her profile both to aid and the women's organisations created under the communist regime, all anathema to the religious movement. Yet while the Taliban's prescriptions on women remained unnegotiable, the widow provided the basis for an embryonic *lingua franca* between it and the international community.

'There is a sense here,' said Leslie in February, 'that the current authorities, like others before them, have manipulated the issue of widows for their own ends. For the time being, this seems to work for both sides. The issue of women's rights has been kept safely distinct from the relief needs, both by the international community and the Taliban.'

That distinction had a lengthy pedigree. In November 1995, two months after Herat fell, UNICEF had announced the suspension of all assistance to education in Taliban-controlled regions of the country, arguing that its ban on girls' attendance at schools constituted a breach of the Convention of the Rights of the Child. It was the first apparent attempt to set a policy benchmark in the long shadow of the controversial Beijing women's conference earlier in the year. Save the Children (UK) followed suit four months later, giving the reason that the ban on employing Afghan female staff made it impossible to communicate with women, the main carers for children.

But this gesture of gender correctness was not entirely of UNICEF's making. Pamela Collett of Save the Children Fund (US), and a doyenne of women's literacy programmes, had leaked details of the organisation's initial appeasement of the Taliban's gender *diktat* to the *New York Times* on 10 November. Peter Hansen, then-head of the UN's Department of Humanitarian Affairs, conceded that Afghan women aid workers did indeed risk losing their jobs under the new dispensation and spoke of the 'terrible dilemma' facing agencies in Taliban-controlled provinces.

Hours later, UNICEF's chief executive, Carol Bellamy, announced the freeze on school projects, but this was more an exercise in damage limitation, than a coordinated response by the UN system to its first challenge over gender apartheid. For the Taliban's decrees had tainted every stratum of an aid effort mandated on equality of access, from the provision of relief and drinking water to the fundamental area of health care, the only sector where women were still permitted to work. Drawing the line at education was sophistry.

UNHCR was already considering the ethics of repatriating refugees to a country where basic human rights were denied to half the population. Indeed, Afghans had reached the same conclusion: returnees dwindled to 11,000 in the first five months of 1997, compared to 121,000 in the preceding year. NGOs tried to assess the ramifications of what, implicitly, signalled the Taliban's wholesale rejection of attempts to address the structural – read 'religious' – context of women's economic exclusion, in favour of a bottomless reliance on unconditional relief. Development – which for most aid workers is shorthand for the empowerment of women and girls, and essential for the survival of widows – had been effectively outlawed.

And yet still the UN held its fire, arguing that the 'non-confrontational' approach would gradually induce the Taliban to modify its position before the momentum of protest built to such a point that the organisation would be compelled to the brink of the unthinkable: a unilateral break on ethical grounds with a government whose every pronouncement made a mockery of the Convention on the Elimination of All Forms of Discrimination Against Women. Afghanistan had ratified that document one year after the Soviet invasion in 1980.

It need not have worried. What remained of the international women's movement was more exercised by Indian women stepping into bikinis at the Miss World contest, taking place that winter in New Delhi for the first time, than the beatings handed out for dress code violations 1,000km to the north west.

Three months after the fall of Kabul, in December 1996, representatives of 250 agencies had met in the Turkmen capital of Ashgabat to consider a coordinated strategy towards the Taliban. But the meeting triggered a process of collective fragmentation which deepened as UN and NGO agency alike sought to secure the survival of their own programmes within the inflexible charter of the *Amr Bil Marof Wa Nai Az Munkir*.

The overiding concern was the continued provision of food and medical aid. 'We are addressing humanitarian needs,' said the head of ECHO, the EU's relief arm. 'Obviously human rights need to be addressed too, but that is not the work of humanitarian aid organisations. Their job is to keep people alive.'

Any looming confrontation over widows, however, had begun to recede within days of the Taliban settling into the capital. WFP projects were inspected and permitted to continue, so long as men and women were not working together. Female supervisors were appointed, on condition that they had no contact with male staff at their Kabul offices.

It was an inefficient and invidious compromise, for expatriate females would have to be hired to do work usually done by female Afghans, and it drew agencies closer into a collaborative relationship with the Taliban on questionable terms. The material needs of widows and their children had been met, but the remainder of Kabuli women were still locked out from work, school and, by September 1997, all but one city hospital. Reports of suicide attempts by women who dared not leave their homes began to circulate, but no agency felt confident enough to take the lead.

By mid-February this year, the main relief agencies had begun to re-examine the 'widow caseload', with a view to re-defining the criteria for selecting beneficiaries. 'It is demographically impossible,' said Leslie, 'for such large numbers of females to have been widowed, even taking into account the scale of loss of life here in recent years. It will be interesting,' he continued, 'to see the response of the authorities to this. In all likelihood, they will choose to view it as another demonstration of the international community's "lack of committment to Afghan women".' ❏

Michael Griffin is completing a book, Reaping the Whirlwind, *on the Taliban.*

EMMA BONINO

Flowers for Kabul

European Commissioner Emma Bonino talks of her concern for the women of Kabul and her 'Flower for the Women of Kabul' initiative, launched on 8 March, International Women's Day

MG: *In September 1997, you visited the last hospital in Kabul where women were permitted to receive medical treatment. Your film crew was beaten up by the Taliban and you were detained for three hours. What did you expect to find? Why did you go?*

EB: In September 1996, few people were concerned by the Taliban's entry into Kabul: the UN representative in Kabul interpreted the event as 'encouraging'. I said straight away that this was a tragic blow for Afghanistan. No good could come from a regime instituted by a sect of fanatical obscurantists. In view of the nonchalant way in which the international community regarded this martyred country, I decided to make a personal visit. This was to show solidarity with the victims of the civil war and to make sure that European humanitarian aid – for which I am responsible – was being used effectively. I won't hide the fact that it was also an attempt to use the media to draw international attention to a 'forgotten' crisis. The treatment I received from the Taliban demonstrated only too clearly that my doubts had been well-founded.

Amnesty International has testified to the rape and abduction of hundreds of Afghan women by the armed factions. Not a single rape has been reported in Kabul since the Taliban took the city. Haven't they been good for the women of Kabul, at least in this respect?

In my country, Italy, those who supported fascism stressed – and continue to do so – that 'in the time of Mussolini the trains always ran on time'. This is not a reason to support a dictatorship, nor to forget its crimes.

ECHO, the agency which you head, has followed much the same policy as the UN in dealing with the Taliban over gender issues: quiet negotiation, respect for traditional customs and the hope that there will be a change in policy. This has not happened. As the largest donor in Afghanistan, is the EU about to wield the big stick?

ECHO, the European Community's Humanitarian Office, shows the united face of Europe to the world. It has only one goal: to relieve the suffering of 'all the victims of conflicts everywhere'. This is, of course, on condition that we are guaranteed access to all the victims of humanitarian crises and that there is no form of discrimination. ECHO does not get itself involved in politics, it upholds values. As for the European Commission, the executive body of the European Community, I fight because we should not let a regime, that so blatantly and scandalously flouts the UN Charter, evade the diplomatic and political consequences of its acts.

What do you hope to accomplish with the 'Flower for the Women of Kabul' campaign?

The Taliban are as sensitive to international pressure as anyone else. As a result of this campaign, I hope the international community will take issue with the Taliban and demand that they respect human rights; specifically, that they will not deny any of the population access to humanitarian aid.

Why has it taken three years since the fall of Herat to launch this initiative? Do you advocate a unilateral withdrawal of aid agencies from Afghanistan because of the Taliban's abuse of women's rights? What would happen to the poor in this case?

I could have perhaps done more, sooner. Yet, even today, people who denounce the Afghan situation still come up against a wall of indifference and hypocrisy. The withdrawal of humanitarian organisations is not at all what I envisage. Let me say it once more: I want to see the Taliban forced to restore the law in their country. It's not for humanitarian organisations to leave Kabul; rather for diplomats and politicians to return to a capital they would clearly prefer to abandon to its fate.

Weak, poor, aid-dependent and in an endless cycle of violence: isn't Afghanistan rather a soft target? Doesn't lining up women's rights in Afghanistan commit the EU to pressing for women's rights in Saudi Arabia, Bahrain, Kuwait, where their access to employment, mobility and education is also limited?

I come from a radical wing of politics, which has made respect for individual freedoms sacrosanct. The majority of Afghan women don't want to participate in public life? Very well. However, I am concerned about the Afghan women who have acquired rights – to study, work, travel, look after themselves, sit in parliament – and who have had these rights taken away by force. This is backward-looking and unacceptable. It's the reason why Afghanistan, far from being a 'soft target', is symbolic of all those countries where women are still waiting for equality. It is the front line in the fight to defend international law against the abuses and savage extremism of such obscurantism.

You are widely portrayed as a mercurial and ambitious person, keenly aware of the power of publicity. Is the Kabul campaign really good for women as a whole, or just for Emma Bonino?

I am used to fighting to the bitter end for causes I think are just. I will use any legal or morally acceptable means to win the battle. Yes, I have made a large personal investment. I cannot do otherwise. ❏

Emma Bonino is a member of the European Commission in Brussels responsible for humanitarian aid and women's affairs. She was interviewed by Michael Griffin

HASAN NUHANOVIC

Witness to Srebrenica

From April 1993 until July 1995, Hasan Nuhanovic worked as an interpreter and translator for the UN Military Observers (UNMO) and the Dutchbat team guarding the demilitarised enclave of Srebrenica. Here, for the first time, Hasan Nuhanovic tells what happened the day the Serbs arrived to destroy the town, massacre its menfolk and drive their widows into exile

From the first moment of the Serb attack on Srebrenica, the two UNMO officers refused to patrol the area and report what they saw or heard to their superiors. My colleague Emir Suljagic and I tried to persuade them to at least patrol the town, if not the countryside, and report the shelling and injuries among the civilians. Though this was no more than their duty, they refused. In the meantime, we translated at several meetings a day between UNMO, the Dutch liason team and local representatives.

UNMO asked the unarmed local guards at the entrance of the PTT building to count and tell Emir and me of all the explosions in the area. This way they did not themselves need to stand at the entrance which was pretty dangerous.

On the evening of 9 July, UNMO got so scared they tried to leave the office for the Dutchbat camp at Potocari but, having first stopped them, the mayor released them when they began to cry. They took Emir with them, but I refused to go without making sure my family was OK.

While walking to our house, a real adventure because of the intensive shelling, I realised the Serbs were in the suburbs of the town and on the nearest hills. I picked up my younger brother and promised my parents I would take care of him. I left him at his friend's place, just across the street.

During the night of 9 July, the mayor and other local representatives asked me to forward some messages to UNMO on the deteriorating situation, but I had no way of reaching them. The following morning, Emir came on foot from Potocari with a map and walkie-talkie. As the situation deteriorated, he and I reported everything – complete with grid references for the Serb tanks and other positions – by radio to UNMO. When I realised the Serb entry into Srebrenica was imminent, I decided to take my brother with me to Potocari.

I radioed Major De Haan and asked him to arrange for my brother to enter the camp. He said he would try. Rather than wait for a reply, I began walking with my brother. We flagged down a Dutchbat jeep driving from the hills and, surprisingly, the soldiers made space for us.

At the camp, Dutch officers took me to a meeting with local officials; they then left me in the Dutch Bravo Coy Camp (about 200 metres from the PTT building). At about midnight, I was called to another meeting in which the Dutchbat commander promised that massive air strikes would take place by 6.00am on 11 July if the Serbs did not withdraw from the borders of the enclave.

I stayed in the Bravo Coy Camp until the morning of 11 July. When it was clear there were to be no air strikes, the Serb bombardment from the hills intensified. Thousands of people gathered in front of the Bravo Coy Camp and, as they broke in through the gate, Serb shells landed in the crowd, killing a couple of people in front of my eyes. The Dutch soldiers dispersed in panic and I decided to run to Potocari to find my brother.

On the way I heard two jets fly over the town, quickly followed by two explosions. When I reached Potocari, along with thousands of other people, the Dutch ordered all the interpreters, about five or six of us, to stand at the entrance and direct people into the camp. After one or two hours the Dutch told us to tell the people that no more would be allowed in, except for some women with babies.

The people looked at us with a mixture of horror and bewilderment. Many still tried to enter the camp but the Dutch soldiers formed a line to stop them. I saw my parents get in and, at that moment, thought they were safe.

I spent the night between 11 and 12 July with one of the Dutch doctors, who claimed he wanted to help people who stayed outside; there were up to 6,000 people inside and about 20,000 around the camp. He helped no-one. There were at least a dozen women with sick babies and others complaining of various problems. Every time they approached the doctor he told them he had no medicine and was there only to help the injured.

On the morning of 12 July, the Dutch were looking for volunteers to represent the 25,000 refugees at a meeting with General Mladic, in Bratunac. My father thought the people wanted him to go because he was an educated man. Three vehicles with the Dutchbat commander and the representatives left the camp for Bratunac. During the meeting, the Serbs completely encircled the camp.

When my father returned with the other two representatives, they were optimistic. Mladic had promised that everyone would be allowed to go to the Croat-Muslim Federation side. The only condition was that the men would be screened for war criminals. He said the rest would then join their families.

But almost immediately, Mladic came to Potocari with hundreds of buses and trucks and began to separate the men from the women and children. On realising the men could not rejoin their families, everybody panicked. The three representatives and I asked Dutch Deputy Commander Major Franken what was going to happen to the men inside the camp. He said it would be a good idea to draw up a list of all the males aged 16-65. This seemed suspicious, but the list was signed by Major Franken. Meanwhile, I continually tried to persuade UNMO and Dutchbat officers to allow my brother to stay with me. First they promised, then refused and so on.

The deportation outside the camp went on until dark. Although scared, the people inside were happy to be 'safe'. We knew the Serb soldiers had separated the refugees and we had heard rumours they were killing the men, despite the Dutch presence. When I asked Major Franken about this he said: 'Don't spread that bullshit around to create panic. That's only bullshit. The evacuation will be continued tomorrow. Once the people outside are evacuated, those inside will be next.'

My mother fainted a couple of times inside the 'new' UNMO officewhen she heard these rumours. They paid no attention. I was even more surprised that the Médecins sans Frontières coordinator, a German woman, called, I think, Christina, did not even look at her. An

Australian doctor (David?) was standing next to her, but he paid her no attention either. Although none of them were more than one metre away, they behaved as if my mother was a piece of furniture.

I heard Christina ask if UNMO had seen any dead people outside. She was talking about nine dead bodies that were lying outside, but UNMO denied any knowledge of them. I heard them say they had seen nothing.

I really panicked, mostly in fear for my brother, and asked Major André Van De Haan, because he was Dutch himself, to try and convince Major Franken to allow my brother to stay inside with me. He promised to do so.

On 13 July at about 8.00am, the trucks and buses started to arrive, but we saw no men among the people who boarded them. This spread panic among the people inside. At about midday, the Dutch told me the Serb 'evacuation' of the people from outside was finished and that the interpreters should tell people inside to leave the camp in groups of five. We did so, but then I heard another list had been drawn up containing the names of those people allowed to stay inside the Dutchbat camp. The representatives were sitting in the conference room and I went there with my father. We asked Major Franken what was going to happen to the men and he told us he had sent the list of 239 names by satellite fax to 'Geneva, The Hague, and other addresses'. He also said he had shown the list to the Serbs outside the camp and, in his opinion, they would think twice before they hurt people whose names were on the list.

That was the only guarantee he gave to the male refugees inside the camp. He did not even think of trying to keep the men and boys inside. No, there was nothing like that. He just ordered everyone in the camp to leave, without any option. The Serbs, carrying long dirty knives and full combat equipment, stood at the gate; their dogs barked at the refugees who were leaving. Meanwhile, the Dutch soldiers just stood by and watched them take all the boys and men away from their wives, sisters and daughters.

I begged Major Franken to allow my brother to stay with me, but he refused. At about 6.00pm on 13 July 1995, the Dutch ordered my mother, my 18-year-old brother and my father to leave the camp, but Major Franken asked my father to stay because he was one of the three representatives. When my father asked Major Franken to allow my brother to stay with him, Franken refused and now told him to follow his son outside the camp. The last time I saw my family was when they walked through the main gate of the Dutchbat.

That evening, the Dutch received a convoy with food and beer. There was the sound of music to the rear of the camp. They were drinking beer and playing loud music as if absolutely nothing had happened.

The Dutch, like the French, British and US governments, are trying to forget the Srebrenica massacre. They are doing nothing to help us, the families of the missing, find out the truth about what happened to our loved ones. ❑

Hasan Nuhanovic works for the UN in Tuzla.

AHMED BURIC

Nobody cried then

To this day, thousands of women from Srebrenica, now living in the suburbs of Sarajevo, have still not discovered what happened to the husbands who were taken to a 'destination unknown' by the soldiers of Serbian general Ratko Mladic between 11 and 13 July

In the sparsely furnished flat of Kada Hotic, a woman in her 50s, her neighbour Suhreta Jakubovic is the first to speak.

'There isn't a single family in this building headed by a man. All the women here are widows. Our husbands are registered as missing; and we are becoming more and more aware that none of them may be alive. We said our goodbyes on 11 July 1995. They took them to a meadow and made them kneel down, like in a mosque before a prayer. I remember that image so well. And none of us cried then; our men didn't, and neither did we women.'

The two women from Srebrenica talk about the past with much more joy then the present. And how did they live before the war? Suhreta starts. 'I had a flat in Srebrenica, my brother had a house and a coffee shop on the ground floor. We also had a small weekend home in the country. I worked in a battery factory and my husband had a job too. Our life was great and now, you see, I have sunk so low that any day they could throw me out into the street.'

'When the war started,' Suhreta continues, 'it is true there was nothing, but we lived somehow and hoped the situation would calm down. I couldn't believe that we could live without salaries but even then we somehow managed. We lived. There was enough wood for heating, although we had to cut down a forest. Srebrenica lies on several sources of fresh water, and so we had the water too.'

One of the commonest phrases heard in Bosnia is this 'to manage'. It does not mean to live life in all its richness and fullness; it does not even mean 'to live' in the European sense. 'To manage' is to be always on the edge of survival. Suhreta explains what 'to manage' meant in besieged Srebrenica.

'Everybody has their own *nafaka* ('destiny' in Turkish, meaning that each man has reserved for him, by the will of God, the amount of food that will sustain him during his life). My husband Eso, who was taken away by the Serbs, kept and refilled non-refillable plastic lighters. I could buy a kilo of flour for each lighter and then exchange it for other food. People who had a small piece of land or who managed to keep a cow or a sheep would give us milk, cheese or meat. It was a real exchange of goods.

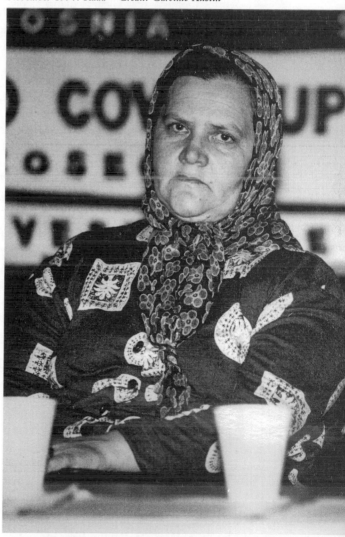

November 1997: Kada – Credit: Caroline Austin

'You probably find it incredible that one could live like that in a town,' Suhreta continues, 'but you'll probably find this even more unbelievable.' Her voice trembles. 'It was better for us during the war in Srebrenica than here and now where I feel that nobody needs us.'

Kada Hotic finds it a lot more difficult to talk about her tragedy. She lost her son, Samir, born in 1966, as well as her brother, her brother-in-law – and her husband. The only one of her family to survive is her daughter, now a refugee in Serbia. 'I still remember the day when they took my husband. I remember we set off in a procession and a Serbian soldier came and started to take away grown men. My husband didn't manage to say anything, he just squeezed my shoulder.' Suhreta adds: 'They say 2,000 civilians went missing that day.'

Kada used to work in a clothes factory before the war; her husband was a chemical engineer. 'I used to sew as well. During the siege, youngsters in Srebrenica started liking a style of 'mini' underpants I sewed, so I had so much work I didn't know what to do first. They would bring me the fabric and I was sewing constantly. That is how I earned the food on which we survived.'

'You know,' Kada continues, 'when you find yourself in a situation where there isn't any electricity or water, and when you've lost all direction, you don't need a clock or anything to remind you that outside that place where you're imprisoned, life goes on: you have neither the time nor energy to think about it. When my neighbour here says that we had it better in Srebrenica then than here and now, it is partly because nobody is doing anything to try and sort out our problems. Only two or three per cent of we women here have found jobs. The rest live on benefits or military pensions.'

Women from Srebrenica have protested to the current Federation government that it is offering them neither a guarantee that they will return to Srebrenica nor any official information about their missing family members. They do not want the Dayton Agreement to be implemented only in Sarajevo because '20,000 people who are not Bosnian Muslims are going to come back and throw us out into the streets again.'

One woman is almost desperate. She says, 'We don't know how to live here. In Srebrenica I had a house, an orchard and a life.' Kada and Suhreta share her view. Suhreta claims: 'Sometimes it seems even logical to me that Sarajevans don't like us much. I'm not sure that I would have liked it if they had come to Srebrenica as refugees and tried to start a new life there.'

Kada adds with tears in her eyes: 'This uncertainty is so difficult to bear. After all we have lost, there's now a chance we'll lose all the help and benefits; that the government will wash its hands of us. The words of the bus driver who drove us from Srebrenica to Tuzla are still ringing in my ears: "Tuzla doesn't want you, Alija (Bosnian President Alija Izatbegovic) doesn't want you. Where am I to drive you?"'

The protest organised on 11 February by the Society of Displaced Citizens of Tuzla Podrinje canton blocked the traffic in the capital all day. Images of women, their faces twisted with pain as they waited to be addressed by someone, anyone, from the government, were beamed into homes all over the world. During the protest, police beat up one unfortunate woman and tension was heightened by the news that their representative and one of the main organisers of the protest meeting, Ibran Mustafic, had been arrested and held in custody.

The level of manipulation is what bothers the women most. 'I was lucky: my sons are still alive. When I was saying goodbye to my husband, we agreed that if they separated us we would try not to betray our marriage: at least one of us would stay alive and look after the children. To my sons I can offer nothing but bare survival. They can only sleep and eat and that is no way to live.'

'Our children are going to work in Holland illegally,' adds Kada, 'and we are waiting to be told what has happened to our dear ones. This treatment is not at all what we hoped for. We have been left to fend for ourselves, we are alone and what we are living is no life at all.'

A telephone rings. Kada says as if to justify herself: 'I'm meeting a friend tonight; we're going to see a play. Do you want to come and see *It Will Be, It Will Be* with us?'

We drove into Sarajevo together, the two of them going on to the theatre. The play, written before the war as a social drama, has been adapted as a comedy and plays to full houses at the Youth Centre. I still haven't seen it because of my misgivings: can you turn a social drama into a comedy? Or is Kada, after all, right? The same helplessness that turns social drama into a comedy turns life into an imitation of life. Kada's and Suhreta's life, however, is not a melodrama; more and more it resembles a tragedy. Yes, I think I shall go and see that production. ❏

Ahmed Buric is a Sarajevo-based freelance writer who contributes to Dani magazine.
For further information: Srebrenica Justice Campaign, C/O Alison Snape, (44) 0181 444 6285.

MALU HALASA

Divided in grief

For 50 years, the Israel-Palestine struggle has created more than its fair share of widows

Women on both sides of the Israeli–War Palestinian divide have seen their menfolk die in the 50-year-long war that began with the creation of the state of Israel in 1948. Widows rank high in the political heirarchy on both sides. Leah Rabin, the wife of the assassinated Israeli prime minister Yitzhak Rabin, and Intisar al-Wazir, better known as Um Jihad, the widow of Abu Jihad, number two in the PLO, have become prominent figures in their own right. Leah is an outspoken, unofficial ambassador for Israel; Um Jihad, elected to the Palestinian assembly in the 1996 elections, was appointed Minister of Social Affairs in Yasser Arafat's cabinet.

Widows like these can also become targets of hostility from their own side. Last summer, Leah was heckled by Orthodox Jews when she visited the bombed Mahane Yehuda Market, while Um Jihad has been criticised for the lavishness of her villa in Gaza. Each woman has impeccable credentials. Leah Rabin met her future husband in the Jewish underground and fought with him in 1948. In the 1960s, Um Jihad ran guns for the PLO. Her husband was gunned down in Tunis in front of her by an Israeli hit squad in 1988.

Israelis and Palestinians both emphasize women's traditional roles as wives and mothers. These political cultures, mirror images of each other, also rely on women's personal courage, and sacrifice.

Originally from Britain **Maureen Benita**, 52, made *Aliyah* – emigrated to Israel – in 1969. She had been working as a nurse among the Bedouins in the Sinai to promote peace through medicine when she met her husband, a medic. He was called up as a reservist in the 1973 Yom Kippur war. After the ceasefire, during a rescue of soldiers in a blown-up tank, his unit was instantly killed when their truck ran over a landmine. Maureen decided to raise her child in Israel. 'Very simply my husband died for the country I lived in. This was the place for our son.' Later he too was wounded after he joined a combat unit. Doubts linger to this day. Maureen learnt of her husband's death after he had been buried for a week in Beersheba. 'I want to tell you something, maybe it sounds queer, but sometimes I think maybe it's not him in the coffin, I've never seen him to say good-bye, so I don't know what's there.'

Uncertainty also bothers **Mirvat Abed**, a 32-year-old mother of five, who lives in Gaza City. Her husband had been teaching at Khun Younis Technical College when a bomb exploded under his car. Mirvat explains: 'The Palestinian Authority arrested Palestinians, but we don't believe they did it. We don't know anything about them, where they're from, why they did it. First I was very sad but after that I want to fulfil my husband's wishes for his children. He was always teaching them how to read their Quran and how to pray when they were young. Always I tell them religious stories. I teach them not to lie, not to steal. They should benefit society, like their father.'

She had been pregnant when her husband was murdered and, as a devout Muslim widow, could have been forced to live with her in-laws. Completely-veiled Mirvat moved out of her husband's family home with her children because of 'the pressure'. She receives a pension from Islamic Jihad. 'All the time my children say that know the Jewish and the Palestinian spies who killed their father, so they want revenge. I agree, those people have stolen our happiness.'

Affa Maffarja, another widow and mother of five from the West Bank village of Beit Lecya, was not allowed to leave her in-laws' home, even to visit her own relatives. Her in-laws also took the money given to her children by the Popular Front for the Liberation of Palestine. Affa became so destitute she sent her three girls to Alyateem, a home for fatherless children in Jerusalem. The public humiliation forced her husband's family to change their behaviour.

Still grieving after four years is **Mary Cohen**, 37, from Beersheba. Her husband Elias, a taxi driver, was shot and killed by members of the PLO, from Gaza, who have never been caught. Mary, a gymnastics coach and folk dance teacher, was so traumatised by the murder she couldn't tell her two children. They were informed by a psychologist. 'I was left alone and the children feel a great emptiness. After the event I hardly

worked. I was at home for almost two years. I'm not political, but I believe that we have to make peace with the Palestinians because all the time people are killed and with peace the killings would stop.'

Thirty-two-year-old **Samar Al-Hidmy** wasn't told of her husband's death. Mustafa, a doctor, was taken in for interrogation by the Israelis, in January 1992. Two weeks later, his parents received a call from the police, asking them to come to the interrogation centre. 'They refused to go. They didn't think he was dead,' recalls Samar. 'They thought the *shabak* (secret police) wanted to use them to put pressure on Mustafa.' That evening, soldiers arrived at the family home and told them their son was gravely ill in hospital. Before Samar could put on her coat, a cousin came and told her not to bother. Suddenly friends started to arrive. 'At that moment I knew Mustafa was dead,' she says.

After a courtcase, Samar won compensation from the Israeli authorities. She lives alone with her son and feels that widowhood has forced her to be stronger. 'I have to solve my problems alone. I told Mustafa when he was alive I would never get a driver's licence. One year after his death, I passed my test. Life has to continue.' She now works in a woman's training programme at the YMCA in Jerusalem.

Tsafi Adorian's husband was injured in the Mehane Yehuda Market bombings in Jerusalem on 30 July 1997 and died 12 days later in hospital. 'If my husband was going to war, to protect his family, for his country, it would be different. But when someone goes to his job and is supposed to come home, you are staring out of the window, waiting for him, listening for the car and suddenly you find him injured in hospital, it's awful. It's taken six months for me even to begin to understand what happened. It is not just the sadness, you react physically.'

Tsafi, a 48-year-old mother of four, has lived in the Jewish settlement of Kfar Adumim on the West Bank for the last decade. 'It is not the West Bank or the other side of the border, but Israel. I wanted to live with religious and unreligious Jews, rich and poor, not in a homogenous community. I would like to live with my [Arab] neighbours peacefully, but it is complicated. There are two people who demand one country. The Palestinians are given all these territories and they bomb us in Jerusalem, they bomb in Tel Aviv. Nobody believes in Oslo. We should have got somewhere in five years.

'You know, we have Bedouin here in the desert. Often I see a woman walking beside the road with a baby in her arms and I am in my car. I know she wants to move more quickly from one place to another. I could take her, but I don't dare. Maybe she would kill me. I can't trust them. It stops you from being a good human being.'

Seventy-two year old widow, and mother of five, **Samiha Khalil** was the only candidate who stood against Arafat in the 1996 elections. She began *In'ash el-Usra*, Reviving the Family Society, in el Bireh near Ramallah, in a garage in 1965. Today *In'ash el Usra* has an operating budget of US$500,000 a month, with vocational, embroidery, practical nursing and beauty centres, as well as nursery facilities and residential child care. Through the work of its members it covers 78 per cent of its operating costs.

Um Khalil maintains self-sufficiency is the key to political change in Palestinian society. 'Instead of helping us return to our lands, UNRWA helped us by distributing dry food, which was not enough either in quality on in quantity. So I decided I wanted every one of my people to be independent.'

Over the years, the society has been closed down innumerable times by the Israeli military and she has been arrested. Her 71-year-old husband died in 1982. She stresses, 'Palestinian widows are taken care of by their sons. For 12 years I had no permission to see my children, nor the permit to let them come and visit me.' Her sons, who had been imprisoned and in the PLO, were returned for the first Palestinian parliament. The work of the society is more important than ever. 'How, when has the occupation changed?' Um Khalil asks. 'Houses are demolished, men are in jail. The people are poor and miserable. We need to ask the Israelis for security; they don't have to ask us. Israel has the money, the weapons.' ❑

*Malu Halasa is a freelance journalist working in London. Samar Al-Hidmy was interviewed by **Khalida Jarrar** of the Addameer Association for Prisoners Support in Jerusalem. She also translated the interview*

Poems from the *Jahiliyya*

AFIRA BINT ABBAD (3RD CENTURY CE)

No one can be as low as the Jadisis who watch the rape of their
brides.
How can a freeborn groom who's given his gifts and dowry put
up with this sting.
He should take his own life rather than see his bride
done in.

AFIRA BINT ABBAD (3RD CENTURY CE)

What's become of you that you let the king rape your brides.
You are as numerous as the ants, yet Afira walks in broad daylight
stained with her virginal blood.
If we were men and you were women we'd stop this crime.
Spark the fire of war and kill the tyrant or be killed, or take to the
wilderness and starve, for it's better to die honourably than live in
shame.
But if you're not moved by this outrage, you might as well bathe
in scent and kohl your eyes and wear the bridal dress.
Death to cowards who strut like men among women.

LAILA BINT LUKAIZ (D. 483)

I wish Barraq had eyes to see the painful state I'm in.
Kulaib, Uquail, Junaid, damn you brothers, I'm your sister, help
me out.
The foreigner lies, he never touched me and I'm still pure, and I'd
rather die than share his bed.
It was you, bastard Anmars and Iyads, who told the Persian fool
where to find me, but my will broke your deal, and bard the sneak
who traded me in went blind with shock.
Banu Acmas, don't cut the Banu Adnan's rope of hope, and if we
hold our ground victory will spring out of despair.
Tell the Banu Adnan I give my life for them
Now rally your men and fly your flags and wave your swords, and
in the sunlight glare march to the Persian lines, and your grit will
turn the battle.
Be alert and ready, O Banu Taghlip, and don't let shame scar your
lives, your sons and the memory of your people.

IMRU AL-QAIS (500-542)

War is a beautiful girl urging young men to sign away their lives.
When the fire bursts into flames, she becomes a friendless old hag
who cuts off her head and offers a broken promise and an
unkissable stinking corpse.

IMRU AL-QAIS (500-542)

I

Stop here so I can roll back the years and cry over the ruins that
housed the girls I onced loved.
The north wind scatters the crumbled walls of my loved girls'
homes and the south wind blows them back, weaving the sight
like a printed cloth.
Oryz dirt like black peppercorns specks the yards and the floors of
the fallen homes.

I feel my tearful eyes burning like a man crushing colocynth seeds
under a samura tree as he watches his loved ones leave at dawn.
My friends pull up their horses and tell me: 'Chin up and don't
wear yourself out with gried. Tears are useless if the ruins can't
reply.
'You're always the same'.
'In another town you loved Umm Harith and Umm Rabab, and
when they walked their scent drifted like a carnation breeze.'
Tears flow down my neck and soak my sword belt.

II

One day at the Darat Juljul pool I met Unaiza and her friends, and
killed my camel for food.
The meat we cooked had lacy frills of fat, which leapt from hand
to hand
I was thrilled as I watched the shapely girls stacking my bundle on
their beasts.
On the way home Unaiza in her swaying hodah said: 'Damn you,
Imrul Qais, you're killing my camel. Get off and walk.'
I teased: 'Relax, my dear, and let your reins go. Stay still so I can
nibble your fruit.
'You're not the first.'
'I've known lots of women, and enjoyed pregnant girls and young
mothers.
'One when her talismanned baby yelled half turned and gave the
brat a nipple while I sucked her other breast.'
'Once I took Fatima to the sand dunes, and when she swore she
wouldn't lift her dress I said: Don't play hard to get.'
'You say I'll die if I don't see you
Break if you must. You think I'll crack ?'
'Too near the knuckle ? Rip the blouse I gave you and we'll call it
a day.
'You only cry so you can shoot pointed tears at my heart.'

III

I've slept with lots of unreachable girls meant to be virgins, and
sidled past the guards who'd have murdered me if they'd had the
chance.
One night the Pleiades spangled the sky like gems and pearls on a
shawl.
I tiptoed into her room and caught her wearing a nightie
'By Allah I can't resist your recklessness, ' she sighed.
Her painted, trailing shift wiped our footprints as we crept round
the square and made our way to the dunes.
There I held the back of her head and felt her fullblooded thrust
She had a firm body the colour of an ostrich egg nourished on
spring water, and her breastbone shone like a mirror.
As she swayed her face I saw her fine cheeks, and her eyes were
soft as a doe watching its fawn.
A necklace burnished her antelope neck, and tresses of charcoal
hair spilled down her spine like bunches of dates on a palm.
Her rope belt rested on legs translucent as dewfilled stems, and
when she got up at noon a cloud of musk rose from her bed.
Her tapered fingers were smooth as scented green twigs, and her
face lit up the night like the oil lamp on a hermit's altar.
Men lose the childhood of love, but my heart never forgets her,
and never grows old.

IV

The night unleashed its blinds like spray and wrapped me in sheets
of worry.
And when it stretched and crouched on me, I pleaded'
'Won't you go ? Though the light is just as harsh, let the day
come'
'Your anchored stars seem tied to a boulder and hitched for
eternity.'

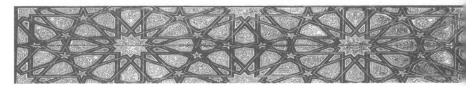

V

While the birds were still in their nests I went out hunting on my
fast galloping horse that catapults back and forth like a boulder
bouncing down a mountain stream.

His back is is smooth a blanket will slip like a raindrop down a
rock.

He's well proportioned and bursting with energy, and when he
runs he snorts like a boiling vat, and races like a shower of rain,
leaving rivals stumbling in the dust.

Quick as a boy's whipped top, he'll buck a novice and crumple
the clothes of a heavy, impatient rider.

He's slim as a deer, swift as a wolf,a nd trots nimbly as a fox.

His long, straight tail centres his flanks, and hsi ribcage curves like
a pestle, or a colocynth seed

We suddenly saw a herd of wild cattle like coloured beads in the
necklace of a lord, and the heifers moved like the gowns of virgins
circling a sacred stone.

While the main herd huddled together we reached the fleeing
steers.

We chased the game without a drop of sweat, and the quarry's
blood splashed and hennaed the stallion's chest, and the cooks
quickly chopped and grilled the raw meat.

There he stood saddle and bridled, my eyes scanning his
handsome form.

VI

Friends, see the lightening flash and rip the clouds like flying
hands, or the sparkling glow of a hermit's freshly lit lamp.
I watched with my friends the lightening streaking across the land
from coast to coast.
A mountain flood swept away a village, uprooted trees so their
grizzled chins hit the ground, and slid into the hideouts of
ibexesx, overturning the palm trees of Taima, and crushing the
brick houses, and only the stone palaces stuck stubbornly to their
ground.
The waters cloaked mount Thabir like a tall lord, and the tip of
the world was a flaxed spindle
The flood threw its cargo onto the plain like colourful cloth out
of a Yemeni merchant's truck
At dawn the birds flew around the valley singing as if they'd
sipped peppered wine, while the drowned beasts lay still like wild
onion tops. ❏

*Translated by **Abdullah al–Udhari**. Abdullah is an Arab poet and
translator from the Yemen, now living in London. These poems are taken
from his forthcoming anthology. They are all from the pre-Islamic era, and
most are banned in the Arab world today.*

Uncaptive Minds

a publication of the Institute for Democracy in Eastern Europe

The most informative journal on Central and Eastern Europe today, featuring politicians, journalists and scholars from the region writing on postcommunist transformation • society • culture • economy • politics.

IN THE CURRENT SPECIAL DOUBLE ISSUE:

The Rise of Nationalism in Eastern Europe and the Former Soviet Union

Secrets of City 19

Forget anthrax and Iraq: far more potent biological weapons exist in City 19, near Sverdlovsk, according to two Russian scientists Lev Fedorov and Seguei Volkov who spoke to the Moscow press in mid-February. The claim was supported one week later by a 1992 defector, Dr Ken Alibek, who told ABC News that the Russian military was still running its biological weapons programme at the site in 1991, one year after Mikhail Gorbachev had ordered it halted.

Volkov was born near City 19, where rumours circulated in the 1980s of a mysterious viral epidemic. On his return in 1993, friends provided documents which led Volkov to conclude that the malady had been caused by a 'super-anthrax' spill in which at least 100 people had died. In 1996, he wrote a brochure about the incident, which was subsequently seized by the police. He alleged then that Boris Yeltsin, the former party boss in Sverdlovsk, had contributed to the original cover-up: the question raised two weeks ago in Moscow was whether the former Soviet Union's biological weapons programme still exists under Yeltsin as president.

Evgeni Toulykine, a military officer who worked at City 19 until June 1996, told *Time* magazine recently that, in his opinion, it does 'even if it is still at an experimental level.' Russia maintains that the centre now performs only civilian research but, despite a 1992 accord with the USA and UK to allow surprise inspections of each others' facilities, no visit to City 19 has yet taken place. However, during inspections of other bio-facilities and depots, US officials have been stunned by the stocks created by the programme. Alibek, the defector, said that the Soviet Union maintained 'hundreds of tonnes' of anthrax bacteria and 'scores of tonnes' of smallpox and plague viruses. The US biological programme was cancelled by President Nixon nearly 30 years ago, although research continues on defensive biological programmes.

In November 1997, the National Academy of Sciences unveiled a $38.5 million US-Russian joint research programme, whose goal, according to director, Colonel Dennis Deplantier, was 'to try to nail scientists to their labs out of fear of proliferation.' The Soviet biological programme employed 9,000 scientists at its height, of whom about half have since left, many for foreign destinations. Was it possible that some had gone to Iraq and Iran? 'I couldn't tell you, even if I knew,' Deplantier told *Newsday*. 'But there is a problem and that's one of the main reasons for going to Russia.'

The question of whether Russia is still working to develop offensive biological weapons is hotly debated by US intelligence. 'We can say Russia continues to research in this area to maintain its military biological potential,' said Alibek. 'They keep safe their personnel, their scientific knowledge and they still have production capability.'

In December 1997 – as Washington announced a new campaign to vaccinate the national cattle herd – the Russian Institute in Obolensk published in the UK magazine *Vaccine* an account of how it had 'genetically modified a strain of anthrax to render it resistant to vaccine.' Despite financing the research under the joint programme, US scientists were unable to acquire a copy of the Institute's methodology.

Meanwhile, another group of US scientists at the National Laboratory of Los Alamos announced on 2 February its own discovery. Using tissue samples taken from the victims of the alleged Sverdlovsk spill 10 years ago, they had isolated 'a form of genetically-modified anthrax, drawn from several different strains,' which was resistant to vaccines suited any individual strain.

All of which sets Russia's strategy during February's US-led confrontation with Iraq over UN access to suspected biological and chemical weapon factories in a more suggestive light. Moscow had taken a leading role in pressing for an end to the crisis through diplomacy, saying it would not accept 'under any circumstances' US air-strikes against its southern neighbour. Yeltsin was supported by France and China in striking this protective pose.

His motive, like theirs, was widely construed as a measure to bring Iraqi oil on stream again, and so recoup some of Moscow's bad loans to Baghdad. But, however recalcitrant Saddam Hussein has and may continue to be under the agreement which Kofi Annan brought back from Iraq, bombing him into submission could have set a dangerous precedent for tracking down and containing other producers of banned weapons. The biological weapons produced in the underground complex at City 19 are likely to put Saddam's secret arsenal to shame. ❏

Michael Griffin

A censorship chronicle incorporating information from the American Association for the Advancement of Science Human Rights Action Network (AAASHRAN), Amnesty International (AI), Article 19 (A19), the BBC Monitoring Service Summary of World Broadcasts (SWB), the Committee to Protect Journalists (CPJ), the Canadian Committee to Protect Journalists (CCPJ), the Inter-American Press Association (IAPA), the International Federation of Journalists (IFJ/FIP), the International Federation of Newspaper Publishers (FIEJ), Human Rights Watch (HRW), the Media Institute of Southern Africa (MISA), International PEN (PEN), Open Media Research Institute (OMRI), Reporters Sans Frontières (RSF), the World Association of Community Broadcasters (AMARC), the World Organisation Against Torture (OMCT) and other sources

ALBANIA

On 28 November in Gjirokastra, four civilians brutally attacked the *Dita Informacion* journalist **Engjell Seriani** who had exposed embarrassing facts concerning the city's water administration. (Albanian Media Monitor)

Head of state television's news department **Enton Alibiblekaj** resigned his post on 20 January, claiming both opposition and government parties tried to influence the work of journalists and interfere in editorial policy. (RFE/RL)

ALGERIA

Salima Ghezali, editor in chief of the banned weekly *La Nation*, was awarded the Sakharov Human Rights Award by the European Parliament on 17 December. (RSF)

Abdelkader Hachani, third-in-command within the Islamic Salvation Front (FIS) was detained for 24 hours on 14 January after he told two French newspapers that foreign governments should press Algeria to open talks with FIS. Hachani was forced to agree not to give interviews for three years after his release from jail in July 1997 (*Index* 5/1997). (*Independent*)

An EU delegation left Algiers on 20 January having been denied access to the village of Sidi Hamed, site of a massacre on 9 January. (*Independent*)

ARGENTINA

Jorge Latana, who was attacked last July (*Index* 9/1991, 2/1992, 5/1997) after his televised report on the privatisation of the state TV network *ATC*, had his contract cancelled by the president's former brother in-law, Emir Yoma, on 2 December. (*Periodistas*)

The newspaper *El Oeste*, of the Esquel Chubut province, suffered an arson attack on its archives and photographic files on 2 December. The editor, **José Agustin Moran Aguilar**, said the attack was probably related to the paper's investigation into several unsolved murders. (*Periodistas*)

On 29 January journalist **Gabriela Cerruti** received an anonymous death threat at her office at *Tres Puntos* magazine. Cerruti is the author of an article in which former Navy Captain Alfredo Astiz expressed no remorse for the disappearances of Argentine citizens during the dictatorship. (*Human Rights Action Network*)

ARMENIA

A week after President Levon Ter-Petrosian resigned, the justice ministry on 9 February removed a ban on the main opposition *Dashnak* party, clearing the way for it to take part in the 16 March presidential election. (*International Herald Tribune*)

Recent Publications: *Summary of Amnesty International's Concerns* (AI, January 1998, 34 pp); *Paradoxes in the Caucasus: A Report on Freedom of the Media in Azerbaijan and Armenia* (CPJ, January 1998, 43 pp)

AZERBAIJAN

On 22 December Foreign Affairs Minister Hasan Hasanov described a Turan news agency report on his recent speech about the conflict in Nagorno-Karabakh as 'anti-governmental'. The following day, Hasanov's deputy minister, Tofik Zulgurov, threatened to ban Turan journalists from questioning ministry employees or entering the ministry building. (RSF)

Salavan Mamedov, editor of the weekly *Istintag,* was arrested and charged on 22 December with criminal libel for allegedly making 'false and dishonouring comments' against Nazim Tagiev, former prosecutor of the Lenkoran district in Baku. Mamedov claimed that Tagiev had cooperated with Alikram Gumbatov, who was convicted of treason and trying to stage an uprising. (CPJ)

In mid-January **Zardusht Alizade**, editor-in-chief of *Istiqlal* newspaper, was taken to the Ministry of National Security where officers threatened to punish him for the 'divulgence of investigation secrets' in articles concerning the former press secretary of President Rasim Agayev who was arrested in November 1996 for high treason. (Human Rights Center of Azerbaijan)

BANGLADESH

On 5 February it was reported that the publisher and editor of the newspaper *Inqilab* feared they were about to be charged with treason. The move followed a statement fom the defence ministry which accused **A. S. M. Baki** and **A. K. M. Bahauddin** of publishing false information about the military with intent to 'damage its reputation internationally' and divide the nation. (BBC World Service)

BELARUS

A justice for the Supreme Commercial Court of Belarus ordered the immediate closure of Minsk-based opposition newspaper *Svaboda* on 25 November. The State Press Commission accused the paper of violating the country's press

law in a series of articles which criticised the administration and compared it to that of Joseph Stalin. The judge cancelled the newspaper's registration and ordered it pay 1 million roubles (approx US$30) to cover court expenses. The paper's editor, **Pavel Zhuk,** said the charges were 'absurd' and represented a warning to other independent and opposition papers. (RFE/RL)

On 23 December, two unidentifed men broke into the studio of renowned film director **Yuri Khashchevatsky** and beat him unconscious, breaking his nose and foot and giving him concussion. No valuables were stolen. Khashchevatsky, a member of the Helsinki Committee and pro-democracy movement Charter 97, made the film *An Ordinary President,* a critical portrayal of the head of state Alyaksandr Lukashenka. It was broadcast on 22 January 1997 by a local cable station in Karelichi, after which local police and State Security Committee officials seized the video and arrested **Maksim Svyrid**, the video operator. Two days prior to the assault, the film was broadcast on the French/German channel ARTE. (HRW)

The trial of journalist **Pavel Sheremet** and cameraman **Dmitry Zavadsky** finally began on 8 January after three postponements. Under Article 80 of the Penal Code they were charged with having illegally crossed the state border *Index* 5/97, 6/97). State prosecutor Vlyadimir Sido requested the court impose two- and three-

year suspended sentences, respectively, but one witness, a border guard officer, said the pair had not crossed the border, as charged. (RFE/RL)

Ihar Hermianchuk, editor of the banned daily *Svaboda*, said he would launch a thrice-weekly newspaper called *Naviny* on 16 January. The paper will have the same editorial content as its predecessor. (RFE/RL)

BELGIUM

Veteran painter Jacques Lacomblez announced in mid-January that he was refusing to lend his collection to Surrealism 98, an exhibition being staged in Brussels to mark the centenary of René Magritte. Lacomblez said the event 'has absolutely nothing to do with the internationalist and subversive spirit of surrealism.' *European)*

BOSNIA-HERCEGOVINA

St George radio, based in Banja Luka and loyal to Bosnian Serb hard-liners, was closed down on 27 November. President Biljana Plavsic's police entered the station during a broadcast on atrocities committed against Serbs in Sarajevo. This is the latest in a series of closures of stations controlled by former president and war crimes suspect Radovan Karadzic. (RFE/RL)

On 27 November, *Alternativa Informativna Mreza* (AIM) editor-in-chief Drazena Peranic called on the international community to clarify the circumstances surrounding the death of AIM journalist **Milorad Ostojic**. According to his family, Ostojic suffered a brain haemorrhage on 28 October after which he slipped into a coma in a Belgrade hospital where he died six days later. Ostojic had written articles critical of local authorities in Teslic and experienced harassment during the municipal election campaign last September. (RSF)

Speaking at a symposium of intellectuals on 29 November, President Alija Izetbegovic rounded on the independent magazines *Svijet*, *Slobodna Bosna* and *Dani*, labelling them 'traitors' and saying they 'spread information contrary to the interests' of the state.(RSF)

Carlos Westendorp, the international community's high representative, announced in Sarajevo on 16 December that a proposed law on Bosnian citizenship would go into force on 1 January. This was the first time he has used powers granted under the Dayton peace accord to impose settlements when Serbs, Croats and Muslims cannot agree on key issues. He has employed the measure to design the new currency and a state flag. (RFE/RL, *Independent*)

The Bosnian Serb Democratic Party's decision to cut live coverage of its new parliament on 27 December provoked international outrage. The Serb wartime leadership cut the broadcast to the northern town of Bijeljina, where the session was being held. The ensuing row blocked attempts by Western-backed President

Biljana Plavsic to nominate a moderate prime minister. (B92)

A spokesman for Carlos Westendorp said on 6 January that the international community intends to appoint someone to supervise the work of Bosnian Serb Television (SRT), based in Plavsic's stronghold of Banja Luka. The decision was taken after SRT aired a virulent anti-Croatian program during Christmas, contravening the ban on the propogation of ethnic hatred. On 7 January, TV Pale announced plans to launch a private station, S Channel. (RFE/RL)

On 16 January some 600 Bosnian Serbs attacked UN police and Muslim politicians in Srebrenica. Exiled former citizens of the town elected a Muslim local administration and mayor last September 1997. (RFE/RL)

On 20 January **Senad Pecanin** journalist, editor-in-chief and owner of weekly *Dani*, was convicted on five charges of slander. He received a two-month suspended jail sentence. **Fahrudin Radoncic**, editor-in-chief of the pro-government daily *Dnevni Avaz,* also plans to seek some US$85,000 in compensation after Pecanin accused him of burning his newspaper's financial records and practising bigamy. (RFE/RL)

BOTSWANA

Caitlin Davies, editor of the now-defunct independent weekly *Okavango Observer*, was due in court on 16 February

charged with 'causing fear and alarm to the public' by publishing a story in 1996 by reporter **Letswetswe Phaladi** entitled 'Terror squad shocks Maun'. The article detailed an outbreak of teenage violence in the north-western town of Maun. They both face two years' imprisonment and a fine. (MISA)

BRAZIL

Marìa Romao, a worker for Globo Television Network affiliate, TV Liberal, decided to flee Maraba in the northern state of Para on 10 December after a series of death threats. Romao reported on the April 1996 massacre in El Dorado de Carajas, where 19 landless workers were killed. The journalist also testified against 153 police officers implicated in the massacre. (*CPJ*)

On 22 December federal court judge Eloy Bernst Justo ordered the closure of the four-month-old community radio station Sambaqui FM, ignoring a ruling by the Supreme Court which determined that it was illegal to seize material from community radios. Radio Sambaqui is the only local media in the area. (*AMARC*)

On 14 January all the equipment of community Radio 98.5FM and documents of the Brazilian Association of Community Radio Stations (Abraco) were seized from their shared offices in Brasilia by representatives of the National Telecommunications Agency (Anatel). The inspectors were accompanied by police who detained two members of the station's staff: Luis Roberto dos Santos, a presenter, and secretary Anarlei Lorenzon. The two were released after posting bail. (*AMARC*)

BULGARIA

Eleonora Gountcheva, journalist for a Sofia sports weekly, requested political asylum in Canada on 17 December. She claimed refugee status having received death threats after publishing articles on corruption and fraud in the country's sports. (RFE/RL)

It was reported on 15 January that **Yovka Atanassova**, editor and journalist with the daily *Starozagorsky Novini*, was fined 1.5 million lev (US$550) under Articles 147 and 148 of the penal code. If the journalist cannot pay, the court is entitled to seize her property. In March 1997 she was given a three-month suspended prison sentence and fined 500,000 lev (US$180) after publishing an article about a lawyer suspected of financial fraud. With two other cases of libel pending appeal, Atanassova faces a jail sentence. (RSF)

BURMA

Satoru Fujita, a reporter for the Japanese newspaper *Mainichi Shimbun,* was deported from Rangoon on 13 January for infringing visa regulations. The reporter had entered without a journalist's visa said the government. (RSF)

CAMBODIA

The decision to expel **Ed Fitzgerald**, the veteran Asia

Business News (ABN) correspondent, was rescinded on 7 January. On 29 December Information Minister Khieu Kanarith had accused Fitzgerald of covering events in a 'systematically tendentious manner' and ordered him to leave the country. The threat was dropped after talks between the government, diplomats and foreign journalists. (Reuters)

On the 8 January the Information Ministry banned six opposition newspapers for 'defaming the country's leaders and threatening national security'. The suspensions were later lifted by Prime Minister Hun Sen in a 'goodwill' gesture to improve the democratic climate. Five editors denounced the suspensions on 10 January as 'dirty tricks' on the part of Hun Sen. (*Phnom Penh Post*)

CAMEROON

On 24 December **Puis Njawe**, editor of *Le Messager*, was arrested at the newspaper's offices. He was later tried for disseminating 'false news' and sentenced to two years in prison on 13 January. He angered the authorities by printing an article by another journalist which questioned the health of President Paul Biya (NDIMA, AI)

The independent *Aurore Plus* was suspended for six months on 21 January. The paper's editor, **Michel Michaut Moussala**, had already been sentenced to six months in prison and fined FF10,000 (US$1,600) on 13 January. On 16 January the paper accused Jean Tchoussa Moussa

Mbatkam, Director General of the National Ports Department of Cameroon (ONPC) and a deputy of the ruling RDPC, of having taken advantage of his position as director of the ONPC to instigate a coup d'état. (RSF)

Also on 16 January, publication director **Samuel Eleme** of the magazine *La Detente* was convicted of 'defamation' charges, sentenced to three years in prison and fined FF10,000. The conviction followed a series of articles in October 1997 that accused John Mandegue Epee, director of a local insurance company, of being involved in theft in Nigeria, before coming to Cameroon as a refugee. (RSF)

CANADA

The federal government formally apologised to the 'First Nations' on 7 January for decades of discrimination, particularly the widespead abuse of aboriginal children at state-funded boarding schools. The schools, some of which operated until the 1970s, alienated thousands of aboriginal and Inuit children from their own cultures and, in the 1980s, prompted a flood of long-ignored complaints of abuse by white teachers and staff. (*International Herald Tribune*, Reuters)

Louise Frechette, the deputy defence minister, was named on 12 January to the post of deputy secretary-general of the UN, as questions about her role in blocking investigations into Canadian human rights abuses in Somalia in 1993 resurfaced.

PIUS NJAWE

In with a rough crowd

I share Cell 15 with about 100 other prisoners, almost all of whom are convicted of murders, assassinations, hold-ups, thefts and armed robberies. My bunkmate, for example, was head of a gang that emptied out my own neighbour's house. In these conditions, my safety is not at all assured.

On 31 December, a group of death-row prisoners invaded the cell, surrounded me and threatened to kill me if I didn't feed everybody in the jail. The reason they gave was that visits had been disorganised by the presence of police forces trying to prevent a public demonstration in my case. I had to use a lot of diplomacy to calm people down.

Violence around me is flourishing continuously. People play poker and drug themselves all day long. The result is constant fighting. The other day, two prisoners knifed each other inches from me. Just before, I was hit by a wooden stick with which one convict tried to beat another inmate. It is not impossible that a similar incident will be deliberately created some day to get rid of me.

While I receive newspapers and books, I don't have the right to write. The prison director called me into his office to forbid it. 'Lift your pencil for as long as you are in jail.' I have stopped writing the 'Convict's Notebook' that I had been publishing in Le Messager since my imprisonment. I now write in secret. I must get up at 3am to write by flashlight, and I must pay my neighbours not to turn me in. This is how I am composing this letter to you.

I am paying for having refused to plunge into the trough. I am paying because every choice must be paid for. But I'm proud of my choice. My only regret is that we still have so many colleagues who think that compromise with the powers that be is the way out. ❏

Pius Njawe, editor of Le Messager, *was sentenced to two years in Douala prison on 13 January for speculating about the health of President Paul Biya of Cameroon in an article on 22 December. He sent this edited message to Paris, where he was awarded the UNESCO/Guillermo Cano Press Freedom prize on 16 February.*

Frechette has been criticised for encouraging Prime Minister Chrétien's government to shut down the Commission of Inquiry into the Deployment of Canadian Forces to Somalia in January 1997 (*Index* 5/96, 6/97,1/98). (*Guardian*)

A Montreal newspaper columnist has angered the city's Japanese community after mocking the 'slanted eyes' of the Japanese in a 9 February column from the Olympic Games in Nagano. Franco Nuovo, a columnist with the French-language daily *Journal de Montréal*, depicted the 'menacing yet slanted eye' of a Japanese customs officer in a column accompanied by a photograph of the writer pulling back his eyelids and hair. (*Reuters*)

CHINA

Days after he sneaked into the country to set up an opposition Justice Party, **Wang Bingzhang**, a US-based dissident, was expelled, it was reported on 10 February. Wang used an alias to obtain a visa and entered via Macau but was seized in Anhui province on 6 February. Two dissidents, **Yang Qinheng** and **Zhang Rujuan**, who have both served prison sentences for underground publishing activities, were detained in connection with Wang's visit but subsequently released. (*Guardian*)

It was reported on 9 February that the Christian activist **Gao Feng** has been released from jail after serving nearly three years. The release comes at the time of a visit by three US church leaders to examine religious freedom. (*Reuters, Guardian*)

Officials reinstated several documentaries to the 1998 Hong Kong Film Festival on 2 February after protests by film directors. The Urban Council had decided to pull 11 films from the April line-up: one was shot by pro-democracy party leader, **Christine Loh**, who is contesting legislative elections in May. (*Reuters*)

A group of poets in Guizhou province were detained on 26 January for planning to launch an independent journal. Hong Kong dissident group, The Information Centre of Human Rights and Democratic Movement, named two of the detained as **Wu Ruohai, Ma Zhe** and **Ma Qiang**. (*Guardian*)

China announced on 12 January it had executed 16 people for murder and robbery during a wave of anti-Chinese violence last year in the Muslim region of Xinjiang. A spokesman for the United National Revolutionary Front of East Turkestan said 13 of the 16 executed were Uighars accused of shouting independence slogans. (*Guardian*)

The director of the foreign affairs office of the *People's Daily* announced editorial changes at the beginning of January. 'In this new year, we want to give this newspaper a new face and give the readers a sense of freshness.' The paper sold 6 million a day during the Cultural Revolution, a figure that has now slumped by half. (*Independent*)

New Internet regulations, unveiled on 30 December, define 'computer crimes' as those which 'leak state secrets' or 'promote political subversion, pornography or violence', and called for fines of up to US$1,800 for providers who violated the rules. Officials cited a need to 'safeguard national security and social stability.' (*New York Times*)

China has granted Rupert Murdoch's News Corps permission to broadcast its Phoenix channel on two cable systems in the Guangdong and Guangzhou Provinces, it was announced at the beginning of January. Phoenix is transmitted in Mandarin but, until recently, could not officially be seen because of the direct-to-home broadcasts of foreign channels. It is estimated that the two systems reach 2.5 million people. (*Independent*)

Five activists were charged in December with disorderly behaviour in a public place, following their arrest on 21 September during a protest march against the annual International Monetary Fund-World Bank meeting in Hong Kong. They accused the government of political censorship and of taking away their freedom of speech. (*Hong Kong Standard*)

COLOMBIA

Four journalists – **Carlos Alberto Giraldo** and **Jesus Abad Colorado** of the daily *El Colombiano de Medellín* and

• •

PANCHEN LAMA

Lions and foxes

'The Tibetan language...has been taken by those foxes who called themselves lions, and toyed with at will and for no reason. This should definitely not have happened...literate people are becoming illiterate in the area of understanding the meaning of words. This is not only a loss to the Tibetan people, but it is also a loss to the culture of the motherland.

'Those who have religious knowledge will slowly die out and religious affairs are stagnating, knowledge is not being passed on. There is worry about there being no new people to train. And so we see the elimination of Buddhism, which was flourishing in Tibet and which transmitted teachings and enlightenment.

'Where, in fact, no rebellion had broken out, when [cadres] wanted to suppress people, they attacked them by falsely accusing and slandering them...Those people who gathered together to chant scriptures, because of their Buddhist religion and for the happiness of mankind, were also regarded as counter-revolutionaries...Cadres did not carry out investigation and study into, but just believed, groundless rumours about 'rebellion is going to take place' and 'rebellion has taken place' and carried out bloody suppression and attacks.

'Because the amount of grain was not enough to feed even those with the lowest requirements, the fire of bitterness and hunger was ignited, and so dregs of fat, grain husks, which formerly were fodder for horses and donkeys, were considered nourishing and fragrant foods. The responsible people in the canteens gathered together tree bark, leaves, grass roots and grass seeds...and made it into a thin gruel, like pig food, and gave it to people to eat... ' ❏

The 70,000 Character Petition, written by the 10th **Panchen Lama Choekyi Gyaltsen***, has been a closely-guarded secret since 1962 when it was first submitted to Mao Zedong. Mao denounced the report as 'a poisoned arrow shot at the Party' and condemned the author, then 24, to nearly 14 years in prison. A Poisoned Arrow was published by the Tibet Information Network, London. in February.*

• •

Carlos Arredondo and **Fredy Ocampo** from a regional television station in Antiquia – were kidnapped on 13 December by the Armed Revolutionary Forces (FARC), together with six local mayors. All were released five days later. The journalists were investigating the abduction of another six mayors from the region. (*RSF*)

Another two media professionals were freed on 18 December by the Jaime Batman guerrilla group. **William Parra**, press secretary for the Colombian president, and **Luis Madolnado** of the privately-owned radio station RCN were held in captivity from 4 December. (*RSF*)

CROATIA

On 4 December legal proceedings against **Davor Buktovic**, a journalist with the weekly *Globus*, began in Zagreb on charges that he had defamed 22 ministers and a former prime minister of the state. The charges arose from a recent article on corruption that was accompanied by a photo of the officials in question. The ministers have also taken out individual suits against the paper for the 'moral harm' they claim was done to them. Buktovic faces up to eight years imprisonment. (RSF)

On 21 December *Feral Tribune* editor **Victor Ivancic** referred to his imminent trial (*Index* 4/96, 6/96, 4/97, 1/98) for 'insulting' President Franjo Tudjman as 'a classic political trial', adding 'the government is trying to criminalise the

fundamental principals of press freedom'. Attacks on the paper were continued by Health Minister Andrija Hebrang, a doctor and hospital administrators in Zagreb, who said they would sue over allegations regarding the deaths of six children in their care. *Feral* currently faces some 50 law suits for damages totalling US$3 million. (RFE/RL)

On 9 January, an unidentified bidder purchased a majority share in the pro-government Zagreb daily *Vecernji List*. A spokesman for independent journalists suspected government supporters of being behind the acquisition. (RFE/RL)

On 21 January Ivana Trump acquired a 33 per cent stake in Split-based daily *Slobodna Dalmacija*, which has the second largest circulation in the state. (RFE/RL)

CUBA

Odalys Curbelo Sanchez was taken in for questioning by two counter espionage and two State Security agents on 9 December. Curbelo, a correspondent for *Cuba Press* news agency, was accused of 'spreading information to foreign enemy radio stations' and of illegally practising his profession, as well as spying. (RSF)

Journalist **Raul Rivero**, winner of a RSF award in 1997, was unable to collect his prize in person on 10 December because of fears that he would not be allowed back from the Paris awards ceremony. (RSF,

Cubanet)

Two Argentine journalists, **Matilda Sanchez** from the newspaper *Clarin* and **Mario Perez Colman** from the daily *La Nación*, were refused visas on 8 January to cover the Pope's visit to Cuba. The Cuban Embassy in Buenos Aires claimed that Sanchez's coverage of Che Guevara's funeral had 'hurt' the Cuban people, while *La Nation* had not respected Cuban immigration laws, since several of its journalists had entered the country on tourist visas to cover stories. (RSF)

Juan Carlos Recio Martinéz, journalist for *Cuba Press*, and **Cecilio Monteagudo Sanchéz**, member of the unofficial Democratic Solidarity Party, stood trial on 3 February on charges of 'enemy propaganda' and 'other acts against state security'. They are accused of producing a leaflet calling on people not to vote in the local elections of October 1997. (AI)

CZECH REPUBLIC

On 5 January **Zdenek Zukal**, owner of the private TV Studio, was charged with making 'biased and false accusations' in a news piece produced for TV Nova's evening news broadcast on 19 November. The item attempted to prove that Vladimir Pryzna, a top police investigator, had accepted a bribe from a local businessman wanted on charges of fraud and currency counterfeiting. Police are continuing their investigation. (CPJ)

A Prague court acquitted ultra-nationalist leader Miroslav Sladek of incitement to racial hatred on 23 January. During a demonstration against the signing of the reconciliation agreement with Germany in early 1997, Sladek said: 'We can only be sorry that during World War II we slaughtered so few Germans.' The court ruled his remarks should 'be judged in the context of his entire speech.' Sladek was immediately released from prison, where he had been detained for over two weeks. (RFE/RL)

DEMOCRATIC REPUBLIC OF CONGO

Early in December in Kinshasa, four journalists working for both foreign and local media were sacked by the state broadcasting network RTNC. The reason given by RTNC's acting head was that they had failed 'to heed instructions... regarding the dissemination of news'. (IRIN)

Mossi Mwassi, a correspondent for the BBC and Deutschewelle, is still being held in detention without charges. He was arrested on 3 December and no explanation for his detention has been given. (RSF)

An RTNC journalist, **Pontien Tshisungu**, was arrested on 6 December, reportedly because of a broadcast on the assassination attempt of Interior Minister Mwenze Kongolo, during a visit to the province of Nord-Kivu and Rwanda. Tshisungu was part of the minister's entourage during the visit. (RSF)

Having been occupied by soldiers for two months, the private Kinshasa daily *Elima* was ransacked on 22 December. Chief executive **Thy Rene Essolomwa** reported that the soldiers had illegally sold the contents of the office, as well as its cars, and had then torn down doors and windows. Since the beginning of December 1997, the offices of the monthly *Moniteur de l'Economie* have also been occupied by the military. Again, no official reason has been given. On 29 December, three members of staff were arrested without charge. (RSF)

Professor Kalele Kabila, an academic and close ally of opposition leader Etienne Tshisekedi, was jailed for two years at the end of January. Professor Kabila was accused of 'propagating false rumours' and was tried alongside journalist **Jean-Francois Kabanda**. Kabanda was accused of publishing 'seditious documents', namely official papers from the Union for Democracy and Social Progress. (RSF)

EGYPT

Ala'a and Gamal Mubarak, sons of the president, dropped their ongoing libel case against six employees of the London-based *al-Sharq al-Awsat* publishing group on 2 December. The defendants had already been sentenced for their roles in producing an unpublished article on the brothers (*Index* 5/1997, 6/1997). An appeal against the convictions had been scheduled for 10 December. (*Cairo Times, Middle East Times*)

December's Cairo International Film Festival brought more than 200 foreign films to the Egyptian public with comparatively little censorship. But Alan Parker's much-vilified *Midnight Express* was one of two films whose screenings were cancelled because they 'conflict with religious values' and 'defame the Arabs'. (*Cairo Times*)

The trial of six editors with the Islamist newspaper *al-Shaab* on charges of criminally libelling former Interior Minister Hassan al-Alfi (*Index* 2/1997, 5/1997, 6/1997, 1/1998) was adjourned until March at a rowdy hearing on 13 December. Alfi claims the paper's campaign to have him removed from office was libellous: *al-Shaab*'s lawyers assert that the action has become meaningless since Alfi's removal from office in the wake of the Luxor killings in November 1997. Improved relations between *al-Shaab* and the government were evidenced on 5 December when President Mubarak publicly embraced the bi-weekly's editor-in-chief, Magdy Hussein. (*Middle East Times*)

The 27 December issue of the London-based daily *al-Hayat* was seized by censors, apparently to prevent distribution of comments by an extremist Islamist. The newspaper contained text from a telephone interview with one of the leaders of *al-Gamaa al-Islamiya*, the group that has claimed responsibility for killing 62 people in Luxor in November 1996. *Al-Hayat* was last seized on 17 September

(*Index* 6/1997). (RSF)

Artistic production police raided the Sina'a Publishing House on 14 January and confiscated 15 copies of two books by **Khalil Abdel Karim**. The books confiscated were *The Yathrib Society* (Yathrib is the pre-Islamic name for the city of Medina) and *The Raaba Songs on the Companions of Prophet Mohammed*. The confiscation, for which no court order has been produced, apparently relates to an eight-month-old ruling from al-Azhar Islamic Research Academy that the books are blasphemous. (Egyptian Organisation for Human Rights, *Cairo Times*)

A new law signed by President Mubarak on 23 January will require cabinet approval for the formation of joint-stock private media companies, including newspapers and satellite broadcasters. The Journalists' Syndicate condemned the law as state interference with press freedom. (*Cairo Times*)

ETHIOPIA

A former journalist with the Oromo-run paper *Urji* and human rights worker **Garoma Bekele** was arrested on 27 October He was taken to court, but still had not been charged with any offence 24 hours later. Meanwhile, **Solomon Namara** and **Tesfaye Deressa**, both journalists with *Urji*, were still being held in detention (*Index* 1/1998) and had also not been charged. (AI)

Four editorial staff, **Biru Tsegaye, Goshu Mogas,**

Taye Belachew and **Antehh Merid**, from the newspaper *Tobiya* were arrested on 16 January. This followed their detention on 12 January where the journalists were released on a bail of 10,000 birrs (US$1,500) each. The newspaper's offices were burnt down a few hours after their second arrest, destroying databases, archive material and office equipment. The police did not want to visit the scene, claiming that they were overworked. (NDIMA)

Berhanu Leyewe, managing deputy editor of Ethiopian weeklies *Keyete* and *Taime Fiqir*, was arrested on 22 January. His whereabouts are unknown. In addition, ex-editor in chief of the weekly *Neka*, **Lulu Kebede**, was arrested and imprisoned in Addis Ababa on 22 January. He is accused of writing and publishing an article in 1995 which criticised the then newly-elected members of parliament. In total, more than 20 journalists are in jail, some of them since 1995. (IFJ, NDIMA, RSF)

Escaped journalists **Nega Tarika Fechisio** and **Andualem Mohammed** fled to Kenya on 10 January after being imprisoned on 'defamation' charges. The writers left on foot without any clothes, money or personal belongings and spent a month at the border, waiting for it to reopen. (NDIMA)

EUROPEAN UNION

Nineteen members of the Council of Europe signed an agreement designed to ban

human cloning on 12 January. Britain and Germany did not approve the protocol which bans attempts 'to create human beings genetically identical to another human being, whether living or dead'. (*Guardian, International Herald Tribune*)

In late January British Home Secretary Jack Straw was said to be considering encouraging greater police monitoring of the Internet during Britain's six-month European presidency (*Index* 1/98). Straw stated that 'we are using nineteenth century procedures to pursue twenty-first century criminals'. (*European, Guardian*)

FIJI

The government approved the drafting of new media regulations on 30 January. A report to the Information Minister Seruwaia Hong Tiy by the British Thomson Foundation recommended the scrapping of the Press Correction Act, left over from the colonial era, and the expansion of the Fiji News Council into an independent Fiji Media Council. The new laws, to be drafted and introduced to parliament for approval, will exclude terms of licensing for magazines and newspapers. (PINA)

FRANCE

In mid-December Jean-Marie Le Pen, leader of the French National Front, repeated the statement he made 10 years previously that the Nazi gas chambers were a 'mere detail' of history, following a drop in his party's opinion poll support.

The last time Le Pen made such a claim, he was fined under the anti-racist laws. (*European*)

A collection of hundreds of newspaper cartoons caricaturing the Jewish army captain Alfred Dreyfus was sold for $20,000 dollars in mid-January. The Dreyfus case, dating back a hundred years, stirred unprecedented levels of anti-Semitism in society at the time. The buyer was Pierre Berge, head of the Yves-Saint Laurent fashion house. (*Guardian, International Herald Tribune*)

GAMBIA

The owner of independent Citizen FM radio, **Baboucar Gaye**, and its news editor, **Ebrima Sillah**, were detained in Banjul on 5 February following a broadcast reporting that the National Intelligence Agency (NIA)'s director of operations had been sacked in connection with an alleged counterfeit scandal. The next day, armed soldiers sealed off the radio station and ordered all staff members to leave the premises. Sillah was released on bail on 8 February, with an order to report daily to the NIA headquarters. Gaye was released on the same bail conditions a day later but rearrested on 10 February after failing to comply with them.(IPI, A19)

GEORGIA

President Eduard Shevardnadze categorically opposes the opening of former KGB archives, according to a report on 9 December. He argued that

opening the archives would give rise to 'a new wave of resistance, mistrust and hatred' and would 'reopen old wounds'. (*Nezavisimaya gazeta*)

GERMANY

In mid-January, a parliamentary committee began an enquiry into neo-Nazi tendencies within the *Bundeswehr* or army. After a series of scandals, Defence Minister Volker Ruhe finally gave into demands for a full investigation when it was revealed that the lawyer Manfred Roeder had been invited to give a lecture to the *Bundeswehr* staff academy in January 1995 on Recolonisation by Russian Germans of the Konigsberg area. The region has belonged to the Soviet Union and Russia since the end of the Second World War. (*European, Guardian, Independent*)

In late January, German Catholic bishops agreed to Pope John Paul II's request that Catholic pregnancy counselling services should be prevented from issuing abortion certificates. The Pope had argued in a letter that such certificates were a 'shadow of ambiguity on the clear doctrine of the church'. Annemarie Griesl-Hillmeier, director of a Munich-based counselling service, complained that 'without the certificates, we will no longer attract the pregnant women who need to be counselled in the first place'. (*European*)

GHANA

Kweku Baako Jr, editor of the weekly *Guide*, may be faced with a charge of criminal libel after publishing a reader's letter alleging that a police task force was in fact a well-equipped commando unit, led by President Rawlings's daughter, Ezanetor. He was called in for questioning by the police CID on 19 January. (Free Expression Ghana)

GUINEA

Louis Espérant Célestin, editor of the independent weekly *L'Oeil* and a Côte d'Ivoire national, was expelled on 22 December. He was accused of 'inciting violence and rioting' after publishing an article quoting a Democratic Opposition Co-ordination party spokesperson saying that the opposition would 'leave no more room' for the ruling Unity and Progress Party. (RSF)

The independent *Le Lynx* and *L'Indépendant* newspapers were closed down on 26 December 1997 and their equipment seized. The security minister said that it was an 'ordinary routine operation' and the equipment confiscated for reasons of public security. (RSF)

Foday Fofana, a Sierra Leonean journalist for *L'Indeépendant* and BBC correspondent, was expelled from Guinea on 7 January after three months' detention in Conakry. Fofana was accused of 'attacking state security' and lying after reporting aggression to a civilian by an assistant commander at a refugee camp.(RSF)

HAITI

On 9 December, **Dely Valet**, director of information for privately-owned radio Vision 2000 and host of *Vision 2000 on Air* was forced into hiding after a plot to kill him was reported. In early December Valet received a death threat by telephone. On 8 December, a group of men linked to former President Jean-Bertrand Aristide entered the offices of Vision 2000 and tried to interrupt the programme. (*RSF*)

INDIA

The Election Commission said on 21 January that the publication or broadcast of opinion polls would be banned for two weeks from 14 February, two days before the general election got under way. Exit polls were also banned from 28 February when the third phase of voting came to an end. (Reuters, United News of India)

The film *Kama Sutra* was finally released nationwide on 6 February after a lengthy battle between the film's distributors, director **Mira Nair** and the censor board (*Index* 4/97, 6/97. The board insisted on six cuts featuring nudity and explicit sex from the Hindi version. (BBC World Service)

INDONESIA

In December Information Minister Hartono warned 15 newspapers to stay within the law and to stop 'misbehaving'. While refusing to name the papers, he told the press in Surabaya that 'as long as they stay within the law, everything will be alright. But if they don't, the law will take its course.' (*Jawa Pos*, Tapol)

Thirteen books by local writers were banned in 1997, according to a report from the Attorney-General's Office. An official declined to name the titles on the grounds that it might encourage readers to seek them out, but activists have compiled the following list: *The People Accuse* by **Muchtar Pakpahan** (*Index* 2/97, 3/97) ; *Indonesia in the Spotlight*: *Primadonna and Primaduka* by **Wimandjaya**; *The 27 July Affair* by the **Institute for the Free Flow of Information**; *Catastrophe in Sumatra* (author unknown); *Mobutu, Suharto, a Sese Seko Phenomenon* (author unknown); *Child of All Nations* by **Pramoedya Ananta Toer**; *East Timor for Beginners* by **PIJAR**; *Bloody Footsteps, Tragedy and Treachery in East Timor* by **Aboepriyadi Santoso**; *I am an Enemy of Suharto* by **Sri-Bintang Pamungkas** (*Index* 4/97); *Crackdown on the Pro-Democracy Movement* by **Asiawatch**; and *New Era, New Leadership* by **Soebadio Sastrasatomo** (*Index* 3/96). Three of the authors – Muchtar Pakpahan, Wimandjaya and Sri-Bintang Pamungkas – currently on trial, as well as the private secretary of Soebadio Sastrasatomo, **Buyung Rachmad**. Rachmad is accused of being instrumental in publishing the book *New Era, New Leadership*, although the author, Soebadio,

has not been charged with any offence. On 14 January Rachmad refused to speak in court until President Suharto appeared as the 'injured party'. Sri-Bintang Pamungkas, a former MP, is still facing charges under the anti-subversion law which carries the maximum penalty of death. In 1995 Bintang was sentenced to 34 months in jail for insulting the president during a lecture tour of Germany. He is still in Cipinang Prison. (TAPOL)

IRAN

Akbar Gandji, journalist with the monthly *Kian,* continues to be held in detention since early December, but no official explanation has been offered for his arrest. (RSF)

The prominent opposition leader **Ebrahim Yazdi**, who was the first post-Shah foreign minister, was released from prison on bail 11 days after his detention on 14 December on the charge of having 'insulted the sacred religious values of the Islamic republic'. He also faces charges of insulting the spiritual leader Ayatollah Ali Khamenei, an offence which carries a jail sentence of up to two years. (AFP)

A total of 197 Tehrani families had their satellite dishes confiscated and now face fines of up to a million rials (US$315) for violating a ban on such equipment. (RSF)

On 28 January **Faraj Sarookhi** (*Index* 6/96, 1/97, 2/97, 3/97, 4/97, 5/97, 6/97, 1/98) political prisoner and editor in

AKBAR GANJI

New fascists, old fascism

'Dr Shariati says a believer is definitely someone who opposes fascism. In other words, a religious person cannot be a fascist...One important point has to be noted here: when fascism was coming into existence in the West, many thinkers were unable to understand the phenomenon. And, today, we are claiming that in our own society, where a fascist movement has been taking shape over the last few years, many thinkers of the left and right are unable to understand it. Thus, it is essential to pose this question: what is the nature of this phenomenon? What is its essence? A phenomenon which some people think is left-wing, because of its fierce anti-capitalist slogans. Is fascism really 'left-wing' or 'right-wing' in nature?

'The fascist movement is a movement that opposes modernity. It opposes modernity and wants to re-create the pre-modern era. However, the question is: Can the pre-modern era be recreated, re-established or reconstructed in the modern world? The fascist movement wants to establish a community, the closed social unit of the past, a feudal society in the modern world. We always find them grieving for a lost past. The 'return to self' is one of their slogans. They speak of the 'golden age' of the past and they want to establish the heavenly era that existed before. But the point is that recreating such a period in the modern world is impossible and such a society cannot be created, especially so using such a modern tool as revolution and ideology. Fascism is a modern movement; it inevitably creates another modern phenomenon known as 'mass society'. To shed further light on the matter, we have to mention another distinction: 'civil society' and 'mass society'.

'Hegel describes civil society as a capitalist society... In such a society, we have a new conception of the human being. What is this new conception? The creation of the individual. In the pre-modern community, we do not have individuals. The individual comes into being in modern society. To establish civil society, we need individuals.

The individual is the source of truth and the creator of values and

● ●

nothing has greater power than the individual. If a person says something new in a pre-modern society, it is considered blasphemy, heresy, apostasy; and the person could easily be put to death. This is not the case in modern society. The value of any individual is greater than that of any idea and an individual cannot be sent to prison or put to death for an idea...

'Order' in mass society is imposed from above, using the instruments of oppression. This kind of order is a product of repression, terror, fear and so on. The opening up of this climate and the blowing of the breeze of freedom would completely wreck this seeming order. The experience of the Soviet Union and the eastern bloc is the clearest testimony to this claim.

'Fascists see all strata, classes, parties and individuals, who are enemies of the fascist movement, as representatives and agents of a foreign power. After melting down individuals and transforming them into drops of water, they dissolve them into the ocean that is the leader...'

Akbar Ganji, *managing editor of the journal* Rah-e Now (New Way), *was arrested on 6 December 1997 and is currently being tried in camera. The charges against him are not known, but his trial is believed to relate to a research paper entitled 'Shariati and Fascism', presented to university students in Shiraz on 10 June 1997. (Dr Ali Shariati was a popular Islamic thinker who spent time in prison under the Shah. He died in 1977.) An edited text of Ganji's paper was published in Teheran in November by the journal* Kiyan *under the title* Satan is the First Fascist

● ●

chief of *Adineh*, was released after serving a one-year prison term. (PEN)

In the first week of February, the Supreme Court rejected **Morteza Firoozi**'s appeal against his conviction and death sentence on charges of 'spying for a foreign country'. At the time of going to press, he faced imminent execution. On 28 January, the official news agency INRA reported that Firoozi, a former editor of the English-language daily *Iran News*, had been sentenced to death. (AI, Reuters)

IRAQ

A former insider in Saddam Hussein's Ba'athist regime, **Saad-al Bazaaz**, has launched a new Arabic-language newspaper, *Al Zaman* (Time), in London. Bazaaz, who defected from Iraq in 1992, was the editor of *Al Jomhourieh* (The Republic), the official Ba'athist party organ. (*Independent*)

ISRAEL

The ministry of internal security arrested two extremists on 21 December who, it said, planned to throw a pig's head wrapped in the pages of the Qur'an into the compound of Jerusalem's al-Aqsa mosque. Avigdor Eskin and Haim Pakovitch had allegedly planned their attack for Friday noon prayers in the holy month of Ramadan, when some 100,000 people attend the mosque. (*Jerusalem Times*)

JORDAN

Playwright **Ali Sneid** was

sentenced to 18 months' imprisonment in late December for violating Article 195 of the penal code by writing an unpublished article that criticised a speech by a local politician (*Index* 6/97). (PEN)

On 26 January the Supreme Court declared the May 1997 amendments to the 1993 Press and Publications law unconstitutional as they were being enforced without ratification by parliament (*Index* 4/97, 5/97, 6/97,1/98). The banning of the 13 newspapers, and actions taken against journalists on the basis of the 1997 amendment, could now be reversed. (Article 19, *Financial Times*)

JAPAN

Jozo Itami, director of *Tampoco* and nine other films, killed himself on 20 December because of a magazine's decision to publish a story claiming he was having an affair with a 26-year-old woman. In a suicide note, he wrote: 'I will prove my innocence by death.' *(IHT)*

The film *Don't Cry Nanjing*, a 1995 China-Hong Kong co-production which depicts the1937 Nanjing massacre in graphic detail, has met with self-censorship in Tokyo where no cinema was willing to screen it. The first showing went ahead on 8 December to an audience of 30 in Nagoya. *(Guardian)*

KENYA

In the run-up to the presidential elections on 29 December, **Koigi wa**

Wamwere had the remaining outstanding conviction against him dropped on 1 December. The writer, human rights activist, former member of parliament and ex-political prisoner stood as candidate for the Kenya National Democratic Alliance Party. (AI)

Njehu Gatabaki, publisher of the Nairobi weekly magazine *Finance*, was abducted by security men on 4 December and subsequently struck several times. He was charged the following day with publishing an 'alarming' article in the 1 December issue of *Finance* entitled 'Moi ordered Molo massacre'. He was also charged with malicious damage and stealing property worth more than US\$27,000. He was released on bail. (NDIMA)

KYRGYZSTAN

On 5 December, the government released order No. 493-p with 'the aim of regulating and improving the quality and contents of advertising through carrying out reform.' The order proposes that, over a one-month period, the authorities remove and ban advertising signs 'which encourage morals and traditions which are alien to the customs and mentality of the citizens of Kyrgystan. (Bureau on Human Rights and Rule of Law)

In mid-January the Oktyabrski District Court of Bishkek heard a complaint against **Irina Stepkicheva**, a journalist from *Nasha Gazeta*. On 15 November Stepkicheva published an article which suggested defence ministry credits have been allocated to a private firm in exchange for financial contributions to a presidential candidate in the 1996 election. The general prosecutor, Asanbek Sharshenaliev, was named in the allegations. In December, Sharshenaliev requested the court to initiate a civil action against the journalist under article 16 of the civil code for 'moral damages', and under article 18 for protection of honour, dignity and business reputation. (Bureau on Human Rights and Rule of Law)

On 20 January the Supreme Court considered the case of **Rysbek Omurzakov** (*Index* 6/97), a journalist from the newspaper *Res Publica*. He was appealing against the 4 November sentence of the Bishkek city court which upheld a lower court decision sentencing him for criminal libel. The Supreme Court found him liable under the civil code. He was fined '100 minimum monthly wages' (US$560). Omurzakov does not have to pay, however, because he had already been granted a presidential amnesty. (Bureau on Human Rights & Rule of Law)

LEBANON

Government efforts to suppress a live television interview with exiled former army commander General Michel Aoun blew up into major embarrassment on 14 December when 63 people were detained during a peaceful demonstration in front of Murr TV in Beirut. Interior Minister Michel al-Murr said the government would 'no longer

allow television to be a place for some people to voice whatever they feel like talking about, especially as it might influence public opinion'. (AI, CPJ)

LESOTHO

Candi Ramainoane, publisher and editor-in-chief of *MoAfrika*, was cleared on 9 January of the contempt charges brought by four cabinet ministers. The judge ruled that an earlier court order did not preclude Ramainoane from publishing statements about the ministers while a defamation suit was in progress. Ramainoane still faces a US$2.7 million defamation claim for publishing stories outlining alleged corruption by the ministers. (MISA)

LIBERIA

On 21 December last year, **Alex Redd**, a journalist with the independent radio station Ducor DC 101, was kidnapped by armed men near Suakoko, 155 km north of Monrovia, on his way back from the funeral of slain opposition leader Sam Dorkie. His tapes, containing evidence of human rights violations in Gbarnaga, were confiscated. On 26 December Redd was charged with 'attempted treason', reportedly because the *Heritage* newspaper wrote about his kidnapping. He was released on bail on 29 December. (RSF)

Managing editor **Forkpa Nyenkan** and journalists **Musue Haddad** and **Stanley Seakor** from the daily *News* were briefly detained by police

on 22 December following an article the same day about the death of a suspect in police custody. (RSF)

On 7 January independent radio station Star Radio was ordered by the ministry of information to stop broadcasting with immediate effect. The station is accused of illegally using two wavelengths, even though the interim government approved their licence on 15 July 1997. (Star Radio, RSF)

On 6 January the public prosecutor, Theophilius Gould, effectively banned the *Heritage* newspaper when he ordered Monrovia's only printing press to stop printing it 'until some problems between [it] and the government had been solved'. A week earlier the paper published an article criticising the government's strained relations with the West African peacekeeping force, Ecomog. (Star Radio, RSF)

MALAWI

On 15 January, 10 Malawian soldiers stormed the offices of the independent *Daily Times* demanding the original transcript of a story by journalist **Kaunland Nkosi** alleging that the rate of HIV was higher in the army than in society in general. The soldiers damaged a computer, smashed a reporter's camera and threatened to kill the journalists if they 'played games with the army'. (MISA)

On 5 February the *Daily Times* was ordered by the High Court to pay politician Ziliro

Chibambo K90,000 (about US$3,000) in defamation costs. The paper stands by its story, published in December 1995, that Chibambo, a former cabinet minister and now ambassador to France, was involved in a brawl with a businessman, known as Thupi, at a Blantyre hotel. (MISA)

MALAYSIA

The editor of *Berita Harian*, a leading daily, was asked to resign for criticising Prime Minister Mahathir's economic policies on 20 December. **Ahmad Nazri Abdullah** had written two editorials which prompted the Supreme Council of Malaysia's ruling United Malays National Organisation to call for his resignation. (*Far East Economic Review*)

MAURITANIA

The Arab-language edition of the independent weekly *Le Calame* was banned on 20 December. Officials from the ministry of the interior retained copies for three days before issuing the final order. It is believed to have stemmed from an article on electoral fraud following the publication of the results of the recent presidential election. The paper had questioned the 'abnormally high turnout, given the fact that the opposition had boycotted the election'. (AI, RSF)

The weekly *Mauritanie-Nouvelles* indefinitely suspended publication on 14 January. Editor **Bah Ould Saleck** and his editorial staff made the decision after the authorities

imposed another three-month ban. The weekly had only recently come to the end of a similar period of suspension, handed down on 2 October. (AI, RSF)

On 17 January three human rights defenders, **Boubacar Ould Messaoud, Maitre Brahim Ould Ebetty** and **Professeur Cheik Saad Bouh Kamara**, were arrested at their homes in the capital. **Abdel Nasser Ould Ethmane**, who lives in France, was charged *in absentia*. The arrests followed a documentary shown on French television about slavery in Mauritania. All four men participated in the programme, and all but Kamara belong to the organisation *SOS Esclaves*. The four were charged with creating a 'non-authorised association' and spreading 'false information'. (AI, RSF)

MONGOLIA

A proposal by the minority faction in parliament to close down the state-owned *Ardyn Erh* and *Zasgiin Medee* newspapers was almost approved at a meeting of the working group on Media Law and Law on Press Freedom on 12 January. 'The main idea of the law is to put an end to the monopoly and to terminate state control over press freedom,' said MP E Bat-Uul. (SWB)

Ten thousand Bibles, confiscated at customs in May1997 under a law restricting the introduction of 'foreign religions', will be released as a sign of goodwill. But 600 videotapes are still

being held because they 'portray Christianity as superior to Buddhism', according to *Ardyn Erh*. (Reuters).

NAMIBIA

Hannes Smith, editor of the weekly *Windhoek Observer*, was imprisoned for four months for contempt of court on 13 February. Smith had failed to produce confidential documents at a coroner's inquest into the 1989 assassination of SWAPO activist Anton Luboswski. (MISA)

NEPAL

Shankar Tanpa, correspondent for the weekly *Naw Aawaj* in Janakpurdham, was jailed on 7 January after reporting that 'corruption was going on in the Janakpur area under the protection of the law'. His press accreditation has been cancelled, and he is believed to have been beaten by police. He is still being detained incommunicado at Jaleswor prison. Subsequently, **Ashok Subedi**, editor of the weekly *Naulo Bihani*, was arrested in Ramechchap on 19 January. The next day **Matrika Pakhrel**, editor of the literary quarterly *Bedana,* was arrested in the central Udayapur district. The latter two were charged with supporting Maoist activities, an accusation their publications have denied. (RSF)

NIGERIA

The poet **Ogaga Ifowodo**, arrested on 6 November last year on his return from the UK, is still being held in solitary confinement without access to family, lawyer or doctors. No charges have been made against him. (PEN)

Oby Eke-Agbai (*Index* 6/97), a regional leader of the Nigeria Union of Journalists, was dismissed on 15 December by her employers, Imo Newspapers Limited, following a 'reorganisation exercise'. Sources believe that her dismissal is another example of harassment for her outspokenness. She was given 24 hours to clear her desk. ('IPR')

Niran Malaolu, editor-in-chief of the privately-owned newspaper *Diet*, was arrested by soldiers on 28 December. No official reason has been given and he is being held in an unknown location. A government spokesman said the order for his arrest had 'come from above'. Night editor **Wale Adele**, sub-editor **Emma Avwara** and **Emeka Egerne**, a technician, were also detained but released the next day without charge. (RSF,'IPR')

Akinwumi Adesokan, novelist and former literary correspondent for the *News*, and its editor **Jenkins Alumona** (*Index* 1/98) were released from detention on 31 December last year. (PEN)

Ben Adaji (*Index* 1/98), a correspondent of the *News* and *Tempo* magazines, was detained on 31 December. No reason has been given and he is being held incommunicado. ('IPR')

Thirty people, including **Batom Mitee**, brother of the self-exiled activist Ledum

Mittee and leader of the Ogoni movement MOSOP since Ken Saro-Wiwa's execution in 1995, were arrested by security forces on 3 January, the day before Ogoni Day celebrations. (AI, Reuters)

Obi Chukwumba, deputy editor of the defunct *African Concord* magazine, was arrested on 5 January by security agents. Reasons for his detention have not been given by the government. **Mohammed Adamu**, a senior journalist (*Index* 5/97, 1/98), and the editor, **Soji Omotunde** (*Index* 1/98), have been detained since 1997. ('IPR')

On 6 January, **Anyakwee Nsirimovu**, executive director of the Port Harcourt-based Institute of Human Rights and Humanitarian Law, and journalist **Tokinbo Awoshalin** of *This Day* newspaper were detained, apparently for reporting on the detentions in Ogoniland. They were released without charge a few days later. (AI)

The offices of an Ibadan-based magazine, *Omega Weekly*, has been under siege since 9 January by security agents demanding to see the editors, without specifiying the reason. The editors have gone underground and the paper has stopped publishing. ('IPR')

Chima Ubani, secretary-general of the Lagos-based human rights umbrella group Democratic Alternative (DA), was arrested by security police on 14 January during a press conference to launch an audio cassette containing testimonies

and opinions of ordinary Nigerians about the political and economic situation in the country. Those attending the launch were threatened with guns and all copies of the tape, *Reflections*, were seized. (AI)

On 8 December the home department of Sindh imposed a ban on the circulation of a Sindhi-language pamphlet entitled *Wahabian, Deobandian ja Kufria Gustakhana Aqaid* issued by *Jama'at Ahle Sunnat*. The ban was imposed under Section 99-A of the code of the Criminal Procedure 1989, which prohibits material likely to foment sectarianism. (*Nation*)

On 10 December, the chief commissioner of Islamabad banned and forfeited a year-old report on the country's human rights situation prepared by the UN's special rapporteur on torture, **Nigel Rodley**. The ban was imposed after an organisation in Indian Kashmir reprinted the report with its own front cover. The ban was ordered on the grounds that this 'literature published in India contains subversive propaganda on the cause of Kashmir'. (*Asian Age*)

On 12 December journalist **Muzaffar Sharma** was shot dead by unidentified men in Shikarpur town. Sharma was associated with Urdu-language daily *Mashriq* (*Index* 6/97). It was reported that Sharma had been receiving threatening letters and telephone calls prior to his murder. (*Dawn*)

Pakistan Television Corporation

and Pakistan Broadcasting Corporation were directed on 13 December to 'allocate reasonable time to the activities of those in politics, but out of the government of the day'. A division bench of the Sindh High Court passed the orders in response to a constitutional position filed by former prime minister Benazir Bhutto. (*Business Recorder*)

On 26 December two journalists working for the Lahore-based Urdu newspaper *Lashkar* – **Irfanul Haq** and **Iftikhar Adil** – were sentenced to six months in prison and fined PR5,000 (US$81) by the High Court in Quetta for reporting the alleged theft of court records. Reportedly, an application was lodged in the incident against the Chief Justice of the Baluchistan High Court and *Lashkar* ran the story under the headline 'Theft Case Against Chief Justice Baluchistan'. Iftikhar Adil was released on 12 January and Irfanul Haq 15 days later. (Pakistan Press Foundation)

On 29 December journalist **Qaiser Mahmood Khokhar** was arrested and beaten by police in Lahore. Khokhar had gone to the police station to collect the discharge papers for a case registered against him on 1 December. He was threatened with death in a staged encounter with police and assaulted. Khokhar was released after his case was brought to the attention of the city's senior superintendent of police. (Pakistan Press Foundation)

On 19 January police raided the offices of the Urdu-language daily *Pakistan* and arrested the editor **Jamil Chishti**, chief news editor **Khalid Farooqui**, senior reporter **Khalid Qayyum**, and reporters **Arshad Ansari**, **Abbas Rauf** and **Ahsan Zia** on charges of 'publishing objectionable material' in the 13 January edition. The article in question was based on excerpts from a classic book, *Sada Bahar*, by Maulana Shibli Naumani, that contained passages which the government thought could inflame tensions between the extremist wings of Shia and Sunni Muslims. Charges were dropped on 27 January. (Pakistan Press Foundation)

Prime Minister Nawaz Sharif promised on 22 January to punish those responsible for the 'tragedy' when East Pakistan broke away to become Bangladesh in 1971. 'There is no doubt that East Pakistan was deliberately separated to keep power in West Pakistan,' Sharif said, adding that he believed the country split because the 1970 electoral mandate of the Awami League party was not honoured. He did not specify whom he blamed for the dismemberment of the country. (*Asian Age*)

Police in Sargodha confiscated newspapers and printing materials from the offices of seven local dailies and their printing presses on 23 January. The newspapers were targeted because they had all printed the verdict of Justice Chaudhry Javed Iqbal which found senior police officers and a magistrate guilty of failing properly to investigate the murder of Tajjamul Abbas, the former commissioner of the Sargodha division. (Pakistan Press Foundation, RSF)

In the early hours of 27 January, Karachi police raided the house of **Raja Tariq**, crime reporter for the Urdu-language newspaper *Jang*. The officers claimed that they had been sent to apprehend a terrorist hiding in Tariq's house. The police beat Tariq's daughter when he tried to ask them about who they were looking for and allegedly stole gold jewellery before they left. Police denied any knowledge of the incident when journalists contacted them about it. (Pakistan Press Foundation).

PALESTINE (AUTONOMOUS AREAS)

The Palestinian delegation to the Arab Writers' Conference, held in Damascus in mid-December, voted to withdraw after the sessions turned into a debate on the merits of the Oslo Accords. The conference had earlier recommended suspending the membership of Palestine. (*Jerusalem Times*)

On 7 January the Palestinian Authority (PA) revoked CBS News' unrestricted access within Palestinian areas. The decision followed the airing on 17 December of a programme alleging government involvement in monopolies selling consumer goods in Gaza and the West Bank. The PA said the programme ignored allegation of Israeli involvement in the monopolies. (*New York Times*)

Simon Davies on

PRIVACY

Patricia Williams on

RACE

Gabriel Garcia Marquez on

JOURNALISM

Edward Lucie-Smith on

THE INTERNET

Ursula Owen on

HATE SPEECH

...all in INDEX

SUBSCRIBE & SAVE

UK and overseas

○ **Yes! I want to subscribe to *Index*.**

❑ 1 year (6 issues)   £39   Save 28%
❑ 2 years (12 issues)   £74   Save 31%
❑ 3 years (18 issues)   £102   **You save 37%**

Name

Address

B8B2

£ _____ enclosed.   ❑ Cheque (£)   ❑ Visa/MC   ❑ Am Ex   ❑ Bill me
(*Outside of the UK, add £6 a year for foreign postage*)

Card No.

Expiry   Signature

❑ I do not wish to receive mail from other companies.

INDEX ON CENSORSHIP

✉ Freepost: INDEX, 33 Islington High Street, London N1 9BR
☎ (44) 171 278 2313   Fax: (44) 171 278 1878
✉ syra@indexoncensorship.org

SUBSCRIBE & SAVE

North America

○ **Yes! I want to subscribe to *Index*.**

❑ 1 year (6 issues) $52   Save 21%
❑ 2 years (12 issues) $96   Save 27%
❑ 3 years (18 issues) $135   **You save 32%**

Name

Address

B8B2

$ _____ enclosed.   ❑ Cheque ($)   ❑ Visa/MC   ❑ Am Ex   ❑ Bill me

Card No.

Expiry   Signature

❑ I do not wish to receive mail from other companies.

INDEX ON CENSORSHIP

✉ INDEX, 708 Third Avenue, 8th Floor, New York, NY 10017
☎ (44) 171 278 2313   Fax: (44) 171 278 1878
✉ syra@indexoncensorship.org

Tatyana Suskin was sentenced by an Israeli court on 8 January to two years' imprisonment for pasting posters in the West Bank that depicted the Prophet Mohammed as a pig (*Index* 5/97). The judge said he had shown leniency because Suskin was 'not completely mentally well'. (Reuters)

A dispute erupted in the Palestinian press after Palestinian-American journalist **Daoud Kuttab** agreed to write a weekly column for the *Jerusalem Post,* beginning 14 January with his diary of his detention by the PA (*Index* 4/1997). *Jerusalem Times* journalist Zainab al-Kurd called Kuttab's decision to write for the right-wing Israeli paper 'nothing less than treason'. Kuttab replied that al-Kurd's article libelled him and said her description of him as a 'collaborator' incited others to violence against him. (*Jerusalem Times*)

Intellectuals and officials marched through Gaza on 19 January to condemn the prosecution in France of **Roger Garaudy**, a French writer accused of denying the Holocaust. Garaudy maintained in his book *The Founding Myths of Israeli Politics* that the killing of Jews during the Second World War amounted to 'pogroms' or 'massacres' and not 'genocide' or 'Holocaust'. The protesters denounced 'Zionist cultural terrorism' as the enemy of free expression. (Reuters)

The PA unlawfully forced the retirement on 19 January of **Qusai al-Abadleh**, the Chief Justice and President of the High Court. His dismissal followed the 17 January publication in the newspaper *al-Risala* of an interview in which al-Abadleh said Justice Minister Freih Abu Medein had 'interfered' with the work of the judiciary. Attorney General Fayez Abu Rameh denounced the decision to force Abadleh's retirement and backed his criticism of the justice minister's interference. (Palestinian Society for the Protection of Human Rights and the Environment)

Recent publications: *Sheer Brutality: The Beatings Continue: Beatings and Maltreatment of Palestinians by Border Police and Police Officers during May-August 1997* (BTselem, August 1997, 36pp); *Out of Jerusalem? Christian Voices from the Holy Land* (Palestinian General Delegation to the United Kingdom, December 1997, 40pp)

PANAMA

Gustavo Gorriti, director of the opposition daily *La Prensa* (*Index* 5/1997, 6/1997,1/1998) and reporter **Rolando Rodrigues** were charged on 20 January with 'slander, insult and falsehood' by Attorney General José Antonio Sossa. In July 1996 the two journalists published an article revealing that Sossa had received a cheque for $US5,000 from a Colombian drug trafficker as a donation to his campaign for re-election to the Attorney General's post. (*RSF*)

PAPUA NEW GUINEA

In an end-of-year summary, **Sean Dorney**, bureau chief of the Australian Broadcasting Corporation (ABC,) described how supporters of Prime Minister Bill Skate had 'continuously attacked' the network's crew during a Christmas tour of the rebel island of Bougainville. ABC recently broadcast secret tapes which allegedly show Skate's involvement in violence and corruption. Dorney also praised local journalists in his report on 5 January. (PINA)

PERU

José Arrieta, former chief of the Investigative Unit of *Frecuencia Latina* of Channel 2 when Baruch Ivcher (*Index* 4/97, 5/97, 6/97) was still the station's owner, is under imminent threat of detention. Arrieta received a notice on 15 December asking him to appear at the Peruvian Anti-Terrorism Agency (Dincote). Arrieta was responsible for the reports of the Canal 2 *Contrapunto* which revealed the torture of former intelligence agent Leonor La Rosa and the assassination of her colleague Mariella Barreto (*Index* 3/97, 4/97, 1/98), cases still under investigation. Another journalist from the programme *En Persona*, **Monica Vecco**, was also summoned in connection with the case. (Institute for Press and Society, RSF)

On 18 December the administration of Andina TV, the last independent channel in Peru, was taken from **Julio Vera Junior** and given to his father, who has strong connections with the Fujimori government. Andina's *En Persona* programme, directed by Cesar Hildebrant (*Index* 4/97,5/97), recruited many of its staff from among the sacked journalists of *Frecuencia Latina* and regularly challenged the government. (*Pulsar*)

On 27 January the Special Court of Terrorism acquitted one civilian and three former soldiers accused of being the 'intellectual and material authors' of the 17 October 1996 bomb attack against Puma, a local affiliate of Global Television and Radio Samoa. Special prosecutor Pedro Ramos Mirando launched an immediate appeal to the Supreme Court, asking for a sentence of 24 years against the accused. (Institute for Press and Society)

POLAND

Prosecutors called in the editor and two other senior employees of the weekly *Wprost* on 15 December. They were released later that day. The authorities claimed they were investigating possible financial mismanagement, while the editors said the actions were designed to intimidate the journal which has been outspoken in its criticism of officials. (RFE/RL)

On 11 December legislators banned sex education as a separate subject in state schools. (RFE/RL)

On 7 January the government granted asylum to Belarusian journalist and Popular Front

activist **Yan Churilovich**. He has been in Warsaw for over a year working on a local newspaper, studying and campaigning against Lukashenka's government. (RFE/RL)

On 12 January, a 13-year-old boy in the northern city of Slupsk was allegedly beaten to death by police. Hundreds of people attended the funeral and his death prompted two nights of rioting, resulting in injuries to protesters, damage to property and over 100 arrests. A revised autopsy showed a blow to the head was responsible for the boy's death and a police officer is being detained in connection with the incident. A federal investigation is to be conducted. (RFE/RL, *European*)

ROMANIA

On 16 December the Senate approved amendments to the education law making the teaching of history and geography in the Romanian language compulsory. It also forbade separate universities in the language of minorities. (RFE/RL)

RUSSIA

On 24 November, police in Dagestan took **Galina Beibutova**, editor-in-chief of *Dagestanskaya Pravda*, to hospital after finding her unconscious on the steps of her house. The newspaper had recently published an article denouncing organised criminal groups active in the republic. (RFE/RL)

Patriarch of Moscow and All Russia Aleksii II expressed concern on 16 December that 'the negative attitude toward the Orthodox Church currently demonstrated by television and the press may herald a new attack on the Church'. He accused television of having a 'communist and anti-religious tone', while private network NTV's broadcast of *The Last Temptation of Christ* (*Index* 1/98) showed contempt. Three days later, the Duma passed a resolution, proposed by LDPR leader Vladimir Zhirinovsky, that accused NTV of 'stoking political confrontation in society', broadcasting 'erotic and pornographic programmes' and ignoring 'the religious feelings of believers.' On 26 December the Duma approved a resolution calling for the government to take legal action against NTV and other television companies and urged government to charge NTV more for the use of state-owned transmission facilities. Yeltsin countered by signing a decree on 21 January ordering equal conditions for all TV and radio companies. (RFE/RL, *Financial Times, Independent*)

On 24 January the *Financial Times* announced, as from April, it would no longer jointly publish *Finansovye izvestiya,* the Russian-language economic news supplement to *Izvestia*. While the paper claimed it wished to develop its US markets, *Kommersant-Daily* speculated that it may have terminated the project in order to remain independent of large holdings, such as LUKOiL and Oneksimbank, *Izvestia's* largest investors. (RFE/RL)

RWANDA

On 28 November **Stephen Smith,** a reporter for the French daily *Libération* was refused a visa by the embassy in France. Modeste Rutabagiro, chargé d'affaires, claimed that Smith 'has only himself to blame, considering the horrors he has written' about the country. (RSF)

On 28 January Rwandan Radio and Television reporter **Wilson Ndayambadje** was beaten and killed by Emmanuel Rutayisirie, a soldier from the national army. Rutayisirie was tried, convicted and executed the next day. (RSF)

Six journalists still remain in prison: **Dominique Makeli,** imprisoned 18 September 1994; **Gideon Mushimiyimana,** imprisoned 17 March 1996; **Joseph Ruyenzi**, imprisoned 30 March 1996; Albert **Baudoum Twizeylmana**, imprisoned 10 May 1996; **Amiel Nkuliza,** imprisoned 13 May 1997; and **Joseph Habyarimana** imprisoned on 28 October 1997. (RSF)

SERBIA-MONTENEGRO

Federal Information Secretary Goran Matic announced on 29 December that no former Yugoslav republic had experienced such a 'media boom' as Serbia. He dismissed EU claims about media restrictions as 'tendentious'. (RFE/RL)

SLOVAKIA

On 3 December Prime Minister Vladimir Meciar announced that press conferences after cabinet meetings were to be discontinued. He added that officials would no longer grant interviews to journalists during state visits abroad unless they were in teams accompanying them. (RFE/RL)

SPAIN

Twenty-three leaders of the Basque separatist party *Herri Batasuna* were sentenced to seven years' imprisonment in mid-December. They were deemed to have collaborated with the terrorist group ETA by allowing three of its members to appear in a 1996 election broadcast. The judges decided that 'the accused gave ETA access to free television time and, by doing so, showed their unconditional support for a criminal organisation that aims to impose its will by terrorising society through violence'. *(European)*

SOUTH AFRICA

On 21 December all eight African-language radio stations at the South African Broadcasting Corporation banned a track from musician **Mbongeni Ngema's** latest CD. The Zulu track, *Ubhuti,* contains lyrics which reprimand a woman for 'killing a man with her vagina'. Ukhozi FM station manager, the first to ban the track, said that Zulu was considered 'too sensitive a language' to use in speaking overtly about sex. (FXI)

The department of housing and land affairs in the Gauteng provincial government has laid charges against a *Sunday* Times journalist, **Elias Maluleke,** and two other persons for the alleged theft of confidential documents. Maluleke wrote an article in 4 January edition alleging that the housing department had flouted government tendering procedures in the appointment of four lawyers to act in an internal disciplinary case. (FXI)

On 14 January officials tried to serve a deportation order on Jean Kanhema, wife of Zimbabwean-born **Newton Kanhema**, a senior journalist for the *Sunday Independent* whose residency is being contested on technical grounds. Newton Kanhema angered the ANC in an interview with Winnie Madikizela-Mandela late last year. She accused the government of reneging on election promises and trying to impose leaders on provincial branches of the ANC. *(Southern African Report,* IPI)

SOUTH KOREA

The trial of **Suh Joo-sik,** representative of human rights group Sarangbang, began on 30 January. He is charged with violating the National Security Law for showing a documentary at last year's Human Rights Film Festival about a 1948 civil uprising on Cheju Island, which authorities claimed was subversive. He was also charged with possession of books which 'benefit the enemy'. (Reuters)

Korean-American reporter **Richard Choi** of Los Angeles-based Radio Korea, was released on 4 January pending trial after spending more than two weeks in a Seoul jail for allegedly slandering the *Korean Times.* The 40-second broadcast, aired on 5 December, discussed the reported financial difficulties of the newspaper and a possible merger between the group and the Hyundai Corporation. The report was not broadcast in South Korea. (CPJ, Reuters)

SRI LANKA

Media Minister Mangala Samaraweera denied on 8 January there was pattern behind recent army raids on Indian journalists in Colombo. The latest took place at the home of **Nirupama Subramaniam,** correspondent for the daily *Indian Express,* on 3 January and marked the third time since mid-November that Indian journalists have been targeted and the fourth since the Liberation Tigers of Tam il Eelam exploded a truck-bomb in Colombo on 15 October. (Free Media Movement, Reuters)

On 5 February the Colombo High Court aquitted **Bandula Padmakumara**, editor of the Sinhalese-language newspaper *Lakbima,* of criminally defaming President Chandrika Kumaratunga. Last July, in a case based on the same alleged incident, **Sinha Ranatunga** *(Index* 5/97), editor of the *Sunday Times,* was found guilty of criminally defaming the president in a February 1995 gossip column. (Reuters)

At approximately 9:00pm on 12 February, *Sunday Times* military

columnist **Iqbal Atthas** *(Index* 10/93, 5/97), his family and servants were attacked by five armed men at his home. Neighbours counted a force of 20 to 25 armed men just outside. Atthas believes the attack came as a result of a series of exposés he has written on military corruption and irregularities in air force procurement. (CPJ)

Recent Publication: *Country Report on Human Rights Practises for 1997 (Bureau of Democracy, Human Rights, and Labor, January 1998, 17 pp)*

SWEDEN

In early January police in Brottby, 19 miles north of Stockholm, attempted to detain about 20 youths at a rock concert featuring the US band Max Resist. The youths had been videotaped giving the Nazi salute, a criminal act. A riot ensued in which 314 arrests were made, not only of nationals but also foreigners from the US, Norway and Germany. Most were released the following day but 25 remained in detention. According to a police spokesman, those giving the salute were guilty of 'racial agitation'. (*Guardian, International Herald Tribune)*

TAIWAN

Taiwan has lifted a ban on rallies and marches advocating secessionism or communism, saying present police powers violated the constitutional guarantee of free speech, the judiciary announced on 24 January. (Reuters).

TANZANIA

The state-run Tanzania Information Service issued a warning on 17 December that it would ban all newspapers and broadcasters carrying 'obscene or comical' cartoons that ridicule the government. (MISA)

Three journalists were briefly detained in Zanzibar on 4 January. Journalists **Mwinyi Sadala** of *Nipashe* and photojournalist **Khalfan Said** of the *Guardian* were detained for three hours at Madema police station after attempting to interview opposition leaders. Sadala's film and camera were confiscated. The same day, police attempted to apprehend BBC correspondent **Ally Saleh**, but he had already gone into hiding. Saleh claims the authorities were angered by the way he had reported events that led to demonstrations in support of detained opposition leaders. (MISA)

On 3 February the Ethics Committee of the Tanzania Media Council ruled that *Majira* and *Nipashe* papers should apologise to members of the public. *Majira* had published a story accusing David Kapinga, chairman of a primary school in Dar es Salaam, of misusing Tsh 5 million (US$8,000). *Nipashe* alleged, incorrectly, that Paul Bomani had withdrawn from elections for the National Executive Committee in Dodoma. The Tanzania Media Council is a self-regulating body which was formed by journalists to improve the media's standards and block efforts to impose any form of external regulation. (MISA)

THAILAND

A proposed law to govern the Internet has ignited controversy, with the Internet Society (IS OC) issuing a letter claiming it would lead to a loss of freedom of expression. The Internet Promotion Act includes many clauses which the ISOC finds contentious. Article 11 and 16 prohibit the exchange of information that 'discredits the nation, government or it's officials' and of issues, such as human rights, which impact on national security. Under the legislation, a provider must be 'well behaved' and not a 'delinquent person under the law'. Four other laws are also being considered: the Computer Security Act, Computer Privacy Act, Electronic Commerce Act and an IT related Anti Trust *Act*. (*New Strait Times, Bangkok Post,* Reuters)

TOGO

A new press code has been adopted by the National House of Assembly. Journalists and editors can no longer be detained until brought to trial and fines have been reduced. New radio and television stations will be designated to the newly-created High Media and Audio-Visual Authority. The new code recommends that at least 51 per cent of radio and television should be controlled by indigenous sources. (*West Africa*)

TURKEY

Erol Anar, former secretary

general of the Human Rights Association, was sentenced on 25 November to 10 years' imprisonment, suspended for five years, for having 'insulted the forces of State Security' in a book entitled *Freedom of Thought* (*Index* 4/95,1/96, 5/96, 6/96). (OMCT)

Two years and 12 hearings later, the trial of eleven police officers accused of the murder of *Everensel* reporter **Metin Goktepe** (*Index* 2/96,1/97, 6/97, 1/98) continues. On 27 November, a new judge, Mustafa Birisik, took over after his predecessor, Kamil Serif, asked to be taken off the trial. Judge Fatma Niljun Ucar, who presided over the 24 July hearing when four police officers were imprisoned, has been Transferred to the Court of Edirne (East Thrace), a move seen as a warning to other judges handling the case. On 8 January a re-enactment of the murder at the crime scene was marred by threats from one of the accused officers to the life of a key prosecution witness. At the 13th hearing on 22 January, the lawyer for officer Battal Kose — who had implicated three superiors in the killing — claimed that his client's statements were caused by 'psychological troubles'. (RSF)

Islamists created a new party, Virtue, in December in anticipation of a banning order on former prime minister Necmettin Erbakan's *Refah* (Welfare Party). The constitutional court ordered the closure of *Refah* on 16 January for violating Turkey's strict secular principles and banned Erbakan from office for five

years. (AFP, *Guardian*)

Imran Akdogan, a 16-year-old boy who sold the Kurdish newspapers *Ozgur Gundem* and *Ozgur Ulke,* was taken by police from his home in Diyarbakir and detained on 11 December. After a week in detention, during which time his family had no news, he was released. (AI)

Himmet Dogan and **Arzu Erkol,** both reporters at the Istanbul office of the far-left journal *Atillm,* were arrested on 17 December in Ankara after attending the trial of a group of students accused of 'insulting parliament'. (RSF)

On 14 January Urfa's Radyo Karacadag was forced off the air for one month The ban was in response to the station's 20 March 1997 broadcast of a debate on Newroz (the celebration of the Kurdish New Year). Another radio station in western Turkey, Demokrat Radyo was suspended for 15 days for its transmissions in support of the Kurdish campaign, One Minute of Darkness for a Permanent Light. (RSF)

Several journalist were attacked on 20 January outside the State Security court in Istanbul. **Faruk Arhan** of the daily *Ulkede Gunde,* **Hulya Topcu** from the daily *Cumhurriyet* and **Ayten Aydin** of the Anatloian Press Agency were attacked by presumed members of the far-right Nationalist Movement Party. (RSF)

Playwright **Esber Yagmurdereli,** whose one

year prison sentence was suspended for 12 months on 9 November, has been ordered back to prison. On 19 January he was directed to return for not having 'complied with legal procedures', although he was not due to return until November 1998. (PEN).

On 23 January a journalist with the *Cumhurriyet*, **Ugur Demir**, was taken for questioning during a rally in Besiktas to commemorate the 1993 killing of another *Cumhurriyet* reporter, **Ugur Mumchu.** During his interrogation, the security forces allegedly said: 'You thought we were going to kill you, didn't you? You thought that you would be the next Ugur Mumchu? You'll write it in your diary'. (RSF)

On 26 January writer **Haluk Gerger** *(Index* 1/95, 5/95, 6/95, 1/96) was jailed for one year in Gudul prison and fined US$1,000 for 'separatist propaganda'. Gerger had written an article in 1993 for the now banned pro-Kurdish daily *Ozgur Gundum* (Free Agenda) criticising the bombing of civilian targets by the security forces. (RSF)

On January 26 a 120-page official report was released which concluded that the previous government had carried out covert operations against the Kurd leadership. The report said that agents had committed murders, worked with drug dealers, laundered their profits through casinos and spent millions of dollars on efforts to assassinate Kurdish leaders and overthrow the government of Azerbaijan.

(International Herald Tribune)

Med TV, the London-based, Kurdish-language satellite station *(Index* 5/97), has been fined £90,000 by the UK's Independent Television Commission (ITC) for breach of its programme code. The penalty was served on 30 January for three breaches of the impartiality requirements and took into account previous breaches. (ITC News Release)

The University of California Los Angeles (UCLA) has refused to allow Ankara to fund a chair in Ottoman studies, because the Turkish government attached conditions to their US$1 million offer that would have forced scholars to ignore the 1915 massacre of the Armenians. *(Independent)*

UGANDA

A recent report by the Uganda Journalists Safety Committee (UJSC) claims that intimidation and attacks on journalists by the government and rebel factions are a common occurence. President Museveni is quoted as saying '...they [the press] think that, when we move on them, the international community will cut off aid. This may hold for now, but there will come a time when we shall not need foreign aid. Then we will move on them.' (UJSC)

UKRAINE

On 1 December **Ludmila Dobrovolskaya, a** journalist with the Odessa television station ART, asked for assurances from President Leonid Kuchma she can

'practise her professional activities' without threat to her personal safety. The appeal came after indications from the regional prosecutor that an attack was planned against her. (RSF)

UNITED KINGDOM

The Freedom of Information Act White Paper, published 11 December, promises greater public access to official documents. Local authorities and quangos will have to make information available and, in some cases, Whitehall will have to surrender civil service advice to ministers previously suppressed under the 'thirty-year rule'. Palace documents remain exempt from the proposed bill. (*Guardian, Independent, The Times*)

Home Secretary Jack Straw intervened in the appointment of the president of the British Board of Film Classification (BBFC) in mid-January for the first time in the ministry's history. Straw vetoed the internal choice, Lord Birkett, possibly as a reaction to the BBFC's passing of two sexually explicit videos in 1997 *(Index* 1/98). Former *Independent* editor Andreas Whittam Smith is to head Straw's desired new team at the BBFC. (*Guardian, Independent, Sunday Times*)

In mid-January, a three-year study in St Helena by the Cheltenham and Gloucester College of Higher Education suggested that there is no direct link between TV viewing and violence among children. TV was first introduced to the island of St Helena in 1995.

The study reveals that the proportion of nine to 12-year-olds experiencing behavioural disorders has not increased beyond its previous level of 3.4 per cent. Tony Charlton of the College stated that 'the argument that watching television turns youngsters to violence is not borne out. This study is the clearest proof yet.' (*Guardian*)

In late January, **Mick Marlow** took his fight for the possession of a manuscript confiscated by West Mercia police to county court level. Marlowe was arrested in autumn 1994 for selling a marijuana growers' manual entitled *Tricameral Sensimilla* through small advertisements in magazines such as *Viz* and *Private Eye*. After six months in prison, Marlowe sought the return of a hard disc containing another work, *Simple Sensimilla*, under the Police Property Act. Droitwich magistrates court ruled against the author on 9 January. (*Guardian*)

On 5 February Prime Minister Tony Blair was quick to deny the Lord Chancellor Lord Irvine's claims that new press privacy laws were inevitable. A spokesman for Blair insisted that 'the Prime Minister's view very strongly is that there will not be a privacy law by the front door or by the back door.' Irvine's statement was made in an interview with the *New Statesman* following press revelations concerning Foreign Secretary Robin Cook's personal life. Late in 1997, gags were used to prevent the *Sun* from revealing the identity of a cabinet minister whose son was involved in a drug dealing incident. (*Guardian, New Statesman*)

USA

The New Year has brought a new, smokeless era in Californian bars. As of I January, smoking is prohibited in all California drinking establishments. Fines for violating the new law are steep – up to US$7,000 for each smoker – and bar-owners themselves are responsible for imposing the fines. The law is the result of 1994 legislation that banned smoking in all of California's workplaces, but temporarily exempted the state's 35,000 bars. (*Economist*)'

A documentary by British filmmaker **Nick Broomfield** about the married life of rock suicide Kurt Cobain and his wife Courtney Love was pulled from Robert Redford's Sundance Festival in Utah over a dispute about the film's content. Lawyers for Love – who has a new career as a Hollywood actress – asserted that Broomfield had not cleared copyright for the film's musical content. The film contains interviews with Love's estranged father and a musician who claims he was offered cash to murder Cobain. Broomfield offered to remove the offending music from the film, but festival officials would not change their minds. (*Guardian*)

Two letters claiming responsibility for an abortion-clinic bombing in late January threatened to continue the violent fight against abortion-rights groups. The letters, said to be from the ultra-right Army of God, said that 'anyone who manufactures, markets, sells' or distributes the French abortion pill RU486 would be targeted if and when the pill becomes available in the US. The Army of God has also claimed responsibility for two Atlanta bombings last year, one at an abortion clinic and the other at a gay bar. (*International Herald Tribune*)

The Justice Department is investigating Microsoft Corp for a second anti-trust violation, adding to the one currently moving through the US District Court. Microsoft is alleged to have violated a 1995 consent decree to encourage more competition in the computer industry. The violation stems from Microsoft's deals with PC manufacturers to install Windows operating systems in their hardware. The practises now under investigation by the Justice Department include 'Vaporware' – pre-announced software updates and releases which, it is argued, illegally discourage competitors from going ahead with their own development programmes. In the past, the Department has found insufficient evidence to mount a Vaporware case, although the investigation commenced in 1995. (Reuters)

Senator Orrin Hatch, Republican head of the Senate Judiciary Committee, warned on 5 February that the 'heavy hand of government regulation' would be needed if any one company were to gain control of the Internet. Hatch said in a speech that Microsoft Corp was trying aggressively to take over the Internet, and that the only way of preventing such a takeover was to pursue anti-trust enforcement, thus pre-empting the need for regulation. (Reuters)

A plagiarism case against DreamWorks and director Steven Spielberg over his film *Amistad* was settled on 9 February. Spielberg had been accused by author Barbara Chase-Riboud of misappropriating the dialogue, plot and characters from her historical novel *Echo of Lions*. In a statement Chase-Riboud recanted, saying 'neither Steven Spielberg nor Dreamworks did anything improper. The judgement was entered in Dreamworks' favour. (*Variety*)

VANUATU

Vanuatu Weekly reporter **Gratien Tiona** suffered facial injuries and photographer **Mark Atnelow** had his equipment smashed when rioters attacked journalists in the capital, Port Vila, on 12 January. Rioters then stormed the government-owned Vanuatu Broadcasting and Television Corporation, which runs the island's only two radio stations, and Television Bilong Vanuatu, warning journalists not to report the disturbances. The rioting arose from revelations about a savings scandal at the Vanuatu National Provident Fund. (PINA)

VIETNAM

On 9 December the interior ministry announced it was to set up a press and information centre with the aim of 'monitoring what is published by the press, particularly concerning security matters, the maintenance of law and order and the constitution of the police force, and compiling reports for leading officials'. (RSF)

The Ho Chi Minh city authorities destroyed 15 metric tonnes of 'poisonous cultural goods' on 11 December. The destruction of magazines, tapes, CDs and books was part of a government campaign against the circulation of 'unhealthy' culture. (RSF)

Also in December it was learned that journalist **Nguyen Ngoc Tan**, who wrote under the name of Pham Thai, is serving an 11-year sentence at the Ham Tan prison camp. Arrested in July 1995, he was sentence on 11 August for 'plotting against the socialist government'. (PEN)

Three journalists from the literary journal *Lang Biang* and of the Lam Dong Province Writers Association have reportedly been placed under house arrest after publishing articles calling for greater press freedom. Since April, **Nguyen Xuan Tu** (pen name Ha Sy Phu), **Bui Minh Quoc** and **Tieu Dao Bao Cu** have been banned from leaving their neighbourhoods, meeting people without permission, had telephones cut off and homes placed under police guard. Their families have also been placed under surveillance. (RSF)

At a media fair held in Ho Chi Minh City on 21 January the new Communist Party chief told editors and journalists to adhere to instructions that were issued in October. Lieutenant-General Le Kha Phieu said the media should be more responsible in implementing the directives. Journalists would also be required to support revolutionary ideology and have a thorough grasp of communist and professional ethics. (Reuters)

YEMEN

On 13 December last **Nabil al-Amoudi,** reporter for bi-weekly newspaper *Al-Ayyam* in the Abyan governorate, was detained by the political security in the town of Zinjibar despite his poor health. His continued detention is believed to be linked to his refusal to heed warnings from security agents that he cease working for *Al-Ayyam* which has published stories critical of government arrests of dissidents. (CPJ)

ZAMBIA

On 19 November, **Reggie Marobe and Abraham du Preez**, TV journalists with the South African Phenyo production company, were expelled from the country as a 'threat to national security'. Accreditation to film a documentary on the ANC, whose headquarters were in Lusaka during the liberation struggle, was revoked. (MISA)

Frederick Mwanza, a freelance journalist detained since 14 November, has been tortured during interrogation over articles critical of the government. He is being implicated in the 28 October coup attempt. Mwanza was served on 2 December with a presidential detention order that allows the police to hold him indefinitely. (MISA, RSF)

On 19 December, *Post* reporter **Mukalya Nampito**, photo-journalist **Sheikh Chifuwe** and a reporter from the *Sun*, **Sandra Mubiana,** were prevented from covering the graduation of senior military officers from a training college. The journalists were told that 'only the government-run media (were) invited to cover the event'. (MISA)

Post reporter **Dickson Jere**, who interviewed former president Kenneth Kaunda the day before the attempted coup and reported his warning to the government of an imminent 'explosion', went into hiding shortly after Kaunda's arrest on 25 December. (MISA)

On 6 January, **Jowie Mwiinga** of Reuters, **Katongo Chisupa** of Agence France Presse, **Musengwa Kayaya** of the Pan African News Agency and **Kalinda Shachinda** of the state-owned *Zambia Daily Mail*, were prevented by police from covering part of the Kaunda case because the court room, including the press gallery, was 'full'. The claim was disputed by journalists inside the court. (MISA)

On 8 January, police barred **Graham Roberston** and **Eddie Taderera,** television journalists from the South African Broadcasting Corporation, and an unidentified Zambia Information Services cameraman, from filming events outside the Lusaka High Court during Kaunda's *habeas corpus* hearing. (MISA)

A new body, the Image-Building and Repair Committee, was established by parliament on 2 December last year to improve the country's image abroad. The committee is chaired by Vernon Mwaanga, a self-confessed drugs smuggler. *(Post)*.

On 27 January, the Lusaka High Court decided not to proceed with contempt of court charges against the *Post's* editor-in-chief, **Fred M'membe**, senior reporter **Reuben Phiri** and human rights activists **Lucy Sichone** and **Alfred Zulu**, until the director of public prosecutions determined whether there was a case to bring. The contempt charges arose from Phiri's 12 January article quoting Sichone and Zulu who called the charges against Kaunda 'cheap'. (MISA)

ZIMBABWE

Gerry Jackson, a presenter with state-owned Zimbabwe Broadcasting Corporation (ZBC), was dismissed on 13 December, accused of 'insubordination and total disregard for authority'. On 9 December, Jackson broadcast news of workers protesting tax increases in Harare on a ZBC Radio 3 phone-in programme and calls from eye-witnesses about police brutality. The programme has been cancelled. (MISA)

Compiled by: Penny Dale, Lucy Hillier (Africa); Andrew Kendle, Nicky Winstanley-Torode, Peter Beveridge (Asia); Simon Martin, Vera Rich (eastern Europe and CIS); Dolores Cortes (south and central America); Rupert Clayton, M. Siraj Sait, Gill Newsham (Middle East); Andrew Elkin (north America and Pacific); Andrew Blick (UK and western Europe).

Central Asia: stepping out

Identities are being undone and remade in the newly independent republics of Central Asia. The once dominant Russians are leaving; Islam is making a comeback, new forms of democracy and of autocracy are evident. Religion remains in thrall to the state and free expression is low on the list of priorities. Meanwhile, the world is knocking at the gates in pursuit of the region's oil wealth

**Compiled by Anthony Richter and David Rieff.
Edited by Irena Maryniak and Judith Vidal-Hall**

DAVID RIEFF

Money, hype and history

For speculators, Central Asia – Kazakstan, Kyrgyzstan, Tajikistan, Uzbekistan, and Turkmenistan, the newly independent states that were collectively known, from the advent of Bolshevik power to the end of the Union in 1991 as Soviet Central Asia – may well be simply just one more emerging market. Great profits can be extracted but the savvy investor understands he needs to get his money in and out quickly. But in Central Asia, there is a difference. 'Less mobile money', as it is called on Wall Street, is in play as well; lots of it. Most of the major western oil companies already have tens of billions of dollars invested in the development of the gas and oil fields, and Russian and Chinese firms have also started to bid aggressively for the rights to exploit the region's hydrocarbon reserves.

The involvement of these multinational energy companies has been less well publicized than it has been in Azerbaijan, in large measure because, despite the threat of spillover from the seemingly endless war in Afghanistan and efforts by proselytising Islamic fundamentalists, the 'political risk' is harder to discern, at least for the moment.

Nor is there the kind of geostrategic balancing act that accompanies the politics of hydrocarbons in the Trans-Caucasus. There is no lobby in the USA demanding fairer treatment for the people of Karakalpakstan in western Uzbekistan, as there is for the Armenians of Nagorno-Karabakh. An investment in Kazakstan, Uzbekistan or Turkmenistan is, well, just an investment, and is unlikely to be on the receiving end of any scrutiny, let alone criticism. The small group of courageous domestic human rights activists, often supported by international human rights groups, have done their best. But this work, while exemplary, has never got much of a hearing either in western Europe or North America.

And for all too understandable reasons. The governments of Central Asia, with the exception of Tajikistan, which has been at war for most of the decade, are repressive. But they have not been murderous in the way that, say, the Nigerian government has been murderous. The calm that the visitor experiences in Tashkent, Almaty or Bishkek may not be the whole story, but it is real enough. People there are certainly not free, and the apparatus of repression remains limber enough, particularly in Uzebekistan. Still, most people in the region would be more likely to complain about their declining living standards than their lack of opportunity for free expression or political choice.

Of course, there is no democracy in Central Asia, but this they rationalise by insisting that it is bound to come, after the market is firmly in place, as, in fairness, it did in South Korea. And the fact that most people in the region are appreciably worse off economically today than they were under Soviet domination is explained away, either by the contention that this is nothing more than the transitory microeconomic 'downside' of a steadily improving economy, or at least, as the most honest among those who make this argument concede, of a stabilising macroeconomic situation. Many of the young men and women who work for US foundations, government-funded 'democracy projects' and 'capacity building' initiatives – two current terms of art – speak excitedly about how, yes, people felt secure in the old system, but they have so many opportunities today.

'Look at all the new shops,' one of these programme officers said to me in Tashkent, pointing at a row of kiosks selling Coca-Cola, vodka, candy and cigarettes. 'The market is taking hold.' The idea that these rather mingy stands represented the first faltering steps of the Protestant ethic and civil society in Central Asia seemed more an article of faith than anything else. 'Yes,' he said. 'People felt safe, but they had no opportunity. Now they have to learn to take risks, the way we all do in the world.'

Better to say that they are at risk. For the 10 per cent or so of the Central Asian population that forms the new political and economic elite, of course things have never been better. Large economic projects are being undertaken, and even some of the ruined infrastructure is being restored to at least a simulacrum of functionality. As in so many parts of the former Soviet Union, it seems as if life has become a great

deal more comfortable if you have money and a great deal less if you do not.

This means that, at least in Uzebkistan, Kazakstan, and Turkmenistan (Kyrgystan is too small and Tajikistan is at war, so they do not really signify in this context), the business traveller can stay in a hotel that is more or less to western standard, rent a cellphone, eat in a proper restaurant and move about freely. The fact that most locals, apart from a very small elite, are in no position to afford a beer in the hotel, let alone spend a night in it, have no use for the cell phone, eat either at home or in traditional tea houses, and can barely move around their own cities without being shaken down by ubiquitous and astonishingly greedy traffic policement is acknowledged by those foreigners who wax so rhapsodic about the region's possibilities, but it is clear that it carries very little weight. The market is a creed, and like all creeds resistant to fact and hostile to scepticism.

For the most part, foreign visitors repeat the same mantra. In Central Asia, they are thick on the ground. Only some are directly on the payroll of the oil companies, but almost to a man they return with the same upbeat message about the region. And their words seem to have at least contributed to investor confidence. Money flows have increased, not just for the development of the gas and oilfields themselves but to improve the infrastructure needed to get the oil and gas to market in the West and for business to operate more smoothly.

Whether these investments will translate into the creation of a market of the type that might actually bring about if not actual political or cultural democracy at least some loosening, is another matter. The type of foreign investment that has been coming in has been more like the kind that is the norm in Sub-Saharan Africa today than the kind that flowed into East Asia a few decades ago. The major cigarette companies are present in force, and their country directors boast that as a market Central Asia, where cigarette consumption is already 150 billion a year, will soon outstrip the USA. But with factories closing, unemployment rising steadily, and all the Central Asian governments either unwilling or unable to maintain either basic social services, the pension system, or the infrastructure of both secondary and higher education, it is hard to see how the freedom to open a kiosk, or, for that matter, the revenues generated by oil and gas leases, will turn Kazakstan or Uzebkistan into the next Asian Tiger economy—as if that threadbare model, in these days of the Asian meltdown, were anything to emulate.

Listening to the Kazak president, Nursultan Nazarbayev, still talking of his country as 'on the threshold of great opportunities,' not the next Asian Tiger, but, as he likes to say, 'a Central Asian Snow Leopard', can be something of an exercise in *déja vu* for those who remember the triumphalist talk that emanated from Nigeria at the height of the oil boom. And, as in Nigeria, the question is what the Kazak government will do with its windfall. Given the leadership in Kazakstan, and in the rest of the region, the outlook is not much better than it was in Nigeria in the 1970s. Corruption in Central Asia is endemic; the Russians, who are far and away the most technically skilled people in all five republics, are leaving or being marginalised; and there is little evidence of any systematic commitment to training a new generation of scientists, managers, and technocrats.

And yet it is difficult to imagine how it could have been otherwise. Few regions of the world could have been less prepared, culturally, materially or psychologically, for independence than the five southern republics of the USSR. The leaders of the independent states were, with one exception, senior Communist Party officials before the break-up of the Union in 1991, and loyal ones at that. Unlike, say, the communist apparatchiks in Federal Yugosalvia in the decade between Tito's death and the wars of Yugoslav succession, the Central Asian communist leadership wanted to go on as before. The reasons for this went far beyond the personal advantage they derived from the Union. For the relationship between the imperial centre and its southern periphery was always far more complex than either Central Asian nationalists or Russians nostalgic for the good old days of the Union like to pretend.

In its heyday, the Soviet Union was both Great Russia writ large and a genuinely multinational, multiethnic state. Central Asia was exploited for its natural resources (cotton in Uzebkistan and Tajikistan, gold and other ores in Uzbekistan and Kazakstan, oil and natural gas in Uzbekistan and Kazakstan) and, at the same time, often received more in terms of development – both in human terms as expressed in things like the expansion of health care and housing, and in terms of infrastructure – than Russia extracted from it.

Moreover, the Soviet Union was more than a country; it was a world. Even today, many people in Central Asia, and not just members of the Russian minority that still live in the region, are nostalgic for it. Some pollsters estimate that, were the matter put to a referendum, more than 50 per cent of the population of the five republics would vote for the recreation of the USSR. Whether this represents a genuine preference or simply a way of expressing despair over the general fall in living standards that has occurred over the past seven years is impossible to say. What is clear is that, for all the new flags, the government pronouncements about a return to the ancient forms and traditions, and vast linguistic and demographic shifts (Russian is being phased out, and Jews, Germans, and Tatars as well as Russians are leaving as quickly as they can), political identity in Central Asia is anything but clear-cut.

It is even possible, though hardly likely, that those who yearn for a return of the USSR will get their wish. Another possibility is that there will be a radical deterioration of the economic situation and, in a political context in which both political freedom and freedom of expression remain virtually non-existent, movements born of despair will arise. Whether they take the form of Islamic fundamentalism, as they would likely do in Uzbekistan and Tajikistan, or manifest themselves in Russian-Kazak ethnic strife in Kazakstan (even today, the Russian population of Kazakstan is more than 35 per cent), or in Uzbek-Kyrgyz ethnic strife in Kyrgyzstan, or even village strife over land and water, such movements might well succeed in undoing whatever stability a combination of state repression and popular passivity have managed to engender in the five republics. Still, the likeliest outcome is not such minor apocalyses but, again as in Africa, grinding, steady immiseration. Even President Nazarbayev, in his otherwise largely triumphalist tract, *Kazakstan: 2030*, conceded as much. 'As a result of the economic downfall [sic],' he wrote, 'we witness obvious detrioration in incomes and in living standards of most of our citizens,' and 'realisation of economic reforms, disintegration of the USSR, and integration of the Kazakstani economy in the system of world economic relations couldn't help resulting in substantial downfall [sic] in volumes of production and consequently...in deterioration of [the] overall social situation.' He adds, 'unfortunately...the middle class [which is] the major support of the state and basic stabilising factor of society...is quite insignificant.'

For all the talk that regularly emanates from American and Western European diplomats about building civil society and genuinely free markets, the reality is that as long as there are no major disturbances to the established order in Central Asia, the great external powers are unlikely to act energetically to encourage a different and more decent outcome. Securing contracts for one's country's companies is increasingly the job of every western diplomat these days, but in Central Asia it often appears as if it is the only job the Western Europeans have much interest in. The Russians, the Chinese, the Americans and the Iranians have real political interests, to be sure. But even their missions are top-heavy with economic counsellors.

And yet it is not just that there is too much money at stake, although there is too much money at stake. The darkest reality of all about western policy is that there is no policy, or, at least, no coherent one. No-one really knows what to do in Central Asia except to pursue their national interests. And these interests are very narrowly construed: extract the oil, build the pipeline, secure the construction contract. The larger strategic dreams, most of which were hatched in Washington in the immediate aftermath of the Cold War and have been kept alive mostly by superannuated retired diplomats and national security officials, in which Uzebkistan was to be wooed away from Russia and turned into the great US ally in the region, and Kazakstan was to be a kind of apolitical oil sheikhdom, have largely been shelved. The brute facts of geography – these countries are far from the USA and close to Russia – and the realisation that, in the post-Cold War, Central Asia was an important region but not a vital one from a US or western European perspective, saw to that. Sooner or later, as Russia recovers, Central Asia will in one form or another again become part of its sphere of influence. In the meantime, there are contracts to be garnered and profits to be made. If the best among foreign diplomats continue to take refuge in ideas about democracies and markets that their everyday experience of the governments in the region must cause them to question, that, too, is understandable. The reality – that there is no Central Asian economic miracle, that there is not even a real market – is too demoralizing in a region that at its best is hardly a cheerful place. And the gloom is deepening.

The current figures are stark enough. Sixty to eighty per cent of the population of Central Asia lives under the poverty line. And mining ventures offer little hope of redressing such inequalities. Extraction industries never, whether in Africa, Latin America or Central Asia, provide enough jobs, at least when compared with manufacturing. Mining mostly helps with the state budget, and does little for the broader economy. Meanwhile, the privatisations, begun with such fanfare and under the approving eye of international financial institutions, have largely amounted to the ruling elite in all five republics dividing up the spoils among themselves. Even western diplomats privately concede the point. The talk of Central Asia's promise, so commonplace two or three years ago, has largely been replaced by discreet silence or off the record consternation as it has become clear that the regimes in power are more interested in remaining in control than in allowing market forces to play freely, even though this too would have exacted a tremendous social cost. If Central Asia's resource base is squandered, as it very well may be, a future closer to Afghanistan's than to Lithuania's looms. The region has already had a taste of this in Tajikistan. All the speeches of rulers like Nazarbayev, or Islam Karimov in Uzbekistan, in which they continue to speak of their countries' shortcomings as if they were not of their own making, cannot change this fact.

Things can always be worse. That is another lesson of the past 10 years. It is already clear that the Asian economic collapse means that Central Asia, realistically, will become even more dependent on Russia, just as the imminent thaw in US-Iranian relations seems to suggest that Washington will be far more circumspect in its relations with the Central Asian republics, particularly with Uzbekistan, which briefly enjoyed American favour precisely because it could be relied on to take an anti-Iranian stance.

The Turks are and will continue to be involved in the region economically, but the fantasies, so prevalent in Ankara half a decade ago, of creating a pan-Turkic economic and political zone from the Golden Horn to the Zaraf Shan mountains, have largely evaporated. As for the Iranians, they are bound by geographical proximity to be concerned with the area, and on ethnic grounds have a particular interest in Tajikistan. But they are realists: Iran understands its limitations in dealing with the Central Asian states.

The Chinese are similarly realistic. They will vie for contracts in the gas and oilfields of Central Asia and make every effort to solidify their relations with Kazakstan so that country makes certain that the Uighur separatists of neighbouring Xinjiang – many of whom live across the border in Kazakstan and like the Kazaks are a Turkic people – find no safe haven there.

The problem for Western European governments, for the USA, and even for Russia is far more complicated. In reality, all are likely to muddle along in Central Asia for the moment unless some extraordinary event like a complete Taliban victory in Afghanistan were to take place – something the USA, Russia and Iran agree must not be permitted to happen.

The Americans are shedding their fantasies slowly, but the process appears to be inexorable. For the Russians, the moment has not yet come when they can formulate a consistent policy toward Central Asia. There are far more pressing internal Russian questions to be dealt with first, and, for the moment, despite the presence of considerable numbers of Russian troops in every one of the five republics except Uzbekistan, and despite the calls of hardliners in the Duma to reestablish the Union, Russia can afford to wait.

What is clear, though, is that when Russian predominance is re-established it will be on very different terms from those that obtained during Soviet times. Russians will need to do little more than maintain order and make money; in short, to practise what in simpler times used to be called neo-colonialism.

Not only will the West not object, there may well be a collective sigh of relief breathed in the chanceries. And the local elites will adapt, just as they did to the Tsars, to Red Power and to the end of the Union and the victory of capitalism. As for ordinary people, unless the times have improved greatly in the interim, it is doubtful that they will care all that much one way or the other. ❏

David Rieff *is a US writer and journalist*

Dos´e is one of the few publications in Russia currently able to speak openly about the fact that freedom of speech is absent in Russia

Ekaterina Degot
Kommersant Daily

Dos'e na tsenzuru

Index on Censorship, In association with the Glasnost Defence Foundation, publish *Dos´e na tsenzuru,* the new Russian-language magazine concerned with human rights and freedom of speech. Each quarterly issue includes articles and reports by writers and journalists from the region, as well as articles translated from *Index.*

The current issue of *Dos´e* features:

*an interview with Mikhail Gorbachev – on the failures of *glasnost* and the new order in Russia.

*a report by Alexei Simonov on the threat to media freedom posed by litigation over 'dignity and honour'

*the hostage diary of Olga Bagautdinova, a journalist kidnapped in Chechnya.

*articles from Index and an expanded *Index Index*

Dos´e na tsenzuru is essential reading for anyone concerned with media and democracy in Russia and its neighbours.

To subscribe

A one year (4 issues) subscription costs £22/$35

Index accepts payment via cheque (in pounds sterling or US$, payable to *Index*), by credit card (Visa, Mastercard or Am Ex), by bank transfer (account number 0635788 at Lloyd's Bank, Hanover Square Branch, 10 Hanover Square, London W1R OBT) or by National Giro through the post office (account number 574-5357 Britain).

33 Islington High Street, London N1 9LH
Tel: (44) 171-278-2313 Fax: (44) 171-278-1878
e-mail: syra@indexoncensorship.org

A8D02

Russia

K

Aral
Sea

Caspian
Sea

Uzbekistan

Turkmenistan

Ashgabat

Iran

Afgh

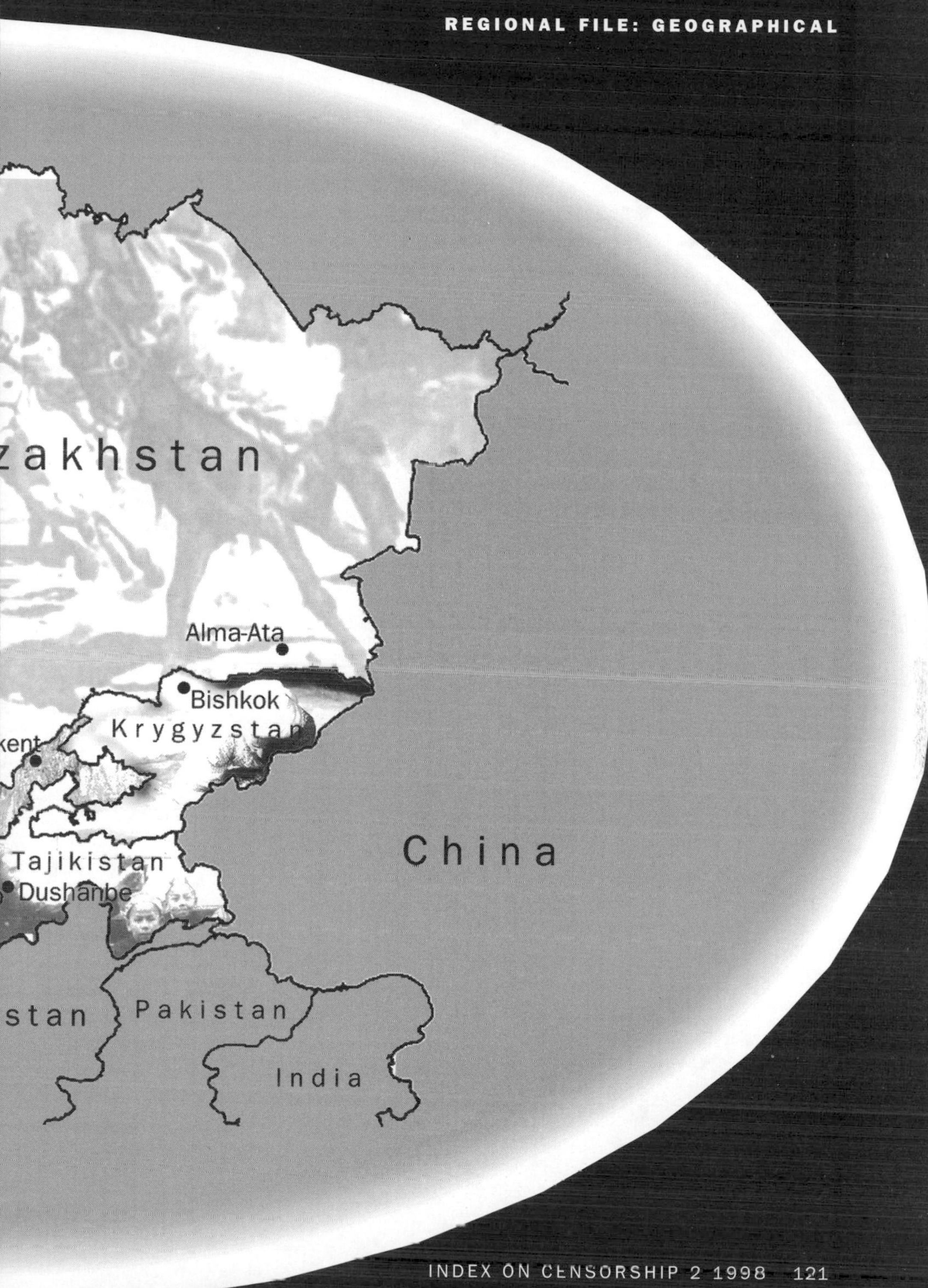

Kazakhstan

Alma-Ata

Bishkok

Krygyzstan

kent

China

Tajikistan

Dushanbe

stan

Pakistan

India

DAVLAT KHUDONAZAROV

Lost worlds

The story of Central Asian photography begins with the conquest of the region by the Russian Empire in the second half of the nineteenth century.

The Russian army's entry into Central Asia was accompanied by a rich display of propaganda. Artists and photographers formed a constituent part of the military campaign. The Emir of Bukhara was defeated and, in 1867, the Turkestan governerate general was created. From the late 1870s, an administrative system was in operation and the infrastructures of cities like Tashkent and Samarkand, which fell directly under imperial rule, began to function. Professional photographers came on the scene.

Their work reflects the tendency of imperial Russian policy not to interfere with or radically change the way of life of local inhabitants. The photographs are stylistically uniform: static group images with symbols or inscriptions indicating their historical significance. Some images (like those of the artist Vereshchagin) emphasised the exotic side of life in the region: the juicy colours of the costumes, poverty and riches, a mythologised cruelty – all this can be sensed in black and white photography as much as in painting. The camera reflects an attraction to the fluent, rounded architectural forms, the mystery of the veil, the unfamiliar bone structures of the faces, all with that same watchful, searching look. The mutual tension and exploration lasted many decades.

Court photographs illustrated official events: the arrival of important figures, including members of the imperial family, the activities of the governor-general and his circle. The innovations that life within the Russian state had introduced (and anything that might strengthen tsarism) were propagated with care, and a kind of tact. In the Turkestan governerate, mainly in cities, the authorities set up Russo-native schools, for local children. In two photographs taken in 1901, one shows a traditional school, the other a new Russo-native one. In the older school, the children have their lessons out in the courtyard, sitting on straw mats. They have no books, and are learning a text orally. It's a

static scene.

The second photograph, showing a Russo-native school, has a stronger internal dynamic. The children are shown in a light, spacious classroom. Its walls are hung with maps and teaching aids. Sitting at their desks, the children listen to the teacher, who demonstrates something to a pupil by the map. But the children are in their national costumes and *tyubeteika* (skull caps). Their traditions have been untouched; they are merely acquiring new knowledge. As far as the authorities were concerned, these were the schools where the future local elite would be trained. The best pupils were sent on to continue their studies at the Tashkent Ostroumovskaya Seminary, named after its founder, a well-known Orthodox Christian missionary.

Shortly after the establishment of the governerates, Russian geographers, historians, ethnographers, anthropologists, botanists and medical researchers arrived to collect data on the newly conquered region. Some had cameras. The policies of the tsarist regime towards the new territories were based on the knowledge they gleaned. Officers on

Dushanbe 1930. A break during the first Tajik Communist Party Congress. Second from the left is Shirinsho Shotemur, who campaigned for recognition of the Tajiks as an independent nation in the early 1920s. He had been elected leader of the Tajik Communists a year earlier and succeeded in making Tajikistan an autonomous republic. At this congress Moscow removed him from his position as leader of the Tajik Communists and appointed its own envoy, the Azeri Mirza Guseynov (second right).

In June 1937, Shotemur was invited to Moscow, arrested in the Metropol Hotel and shot on 29 October 1937. In 1993 it was established that his remains, like those of thousands of others, had been buried in a mass grave in the Danilov cemetry in Moscow.

Furthest right is Ibrahim Ismailov, grandfather of my wife Gavhar. He was shot in early 1938, aged 36.

military service also occasionally showed an interest in the life of the
local population and did their own research. Some, like Andrei Snesarev,
wrote books. In 1901 he became the head of the Pamir border
detachment and took a wide variety of photographs. Most were
unconnected with his professional concerns and served to illustrate
letters to friends and relations, or notes in his diaries. They suggest a
sympathetic understanding of the local population and a real knowledge
of their culture.

At the beginning of the twentieth century a second wave of Russian
academics visited the region. The ethnologist Mikhail Andreyev
described the Pamir as a living laboratory, which gave the opportunity to
study the most ancient strata of Indo-European culture. In 1916, Nikolai
Vavilov was delighted by the skill of Tajik farmers, their sophisticated
systems of irrigation in mountainous territory. The scientists were
anxious to provoke interest in the world to which they had devoted their

lives; their photographs have an authentic and compassionate quality.

The character of the photographic image of Central Asia changed radically after the 1917 revolution. A stable traditional world had been shaken to the core. In 1920, Emir Alimkhan of Bukhara was ousted and the feudal rule of the Mangy dynasty, in power for over a century, came to an end. Photographers became chroniclers. They focused on public meetings, gatherings of the soviets and revolutionary committees, Red

Army parades and groups: soldiers, officials, schoolchildren. The faces speak of enthusiasm and hope, anxiety and bewilderment. Most photographs of Dushanbe in the 1920s were taken by V Medved. He put together official albums on the establishment of the Tajik Autonomous Republic and offers a visual record of the most important events, key figures and atmosphere of that time. He photographed the first government offices, which were small clay shacks, scenes of daily life and, especially, people.

The more subtle propaganda of pre-revolutionary times, when different cultures co-existed in parallel, was transformed under Soviet rule into a head-on confrontation between negative and positive. Every image became a political statement. But even within this crude ideological framework, photographers still worked like artists.

As Soviet power established itself, a canonisation of images followed, and any vestige of the authentic vanished from the official photography of the 1930s. Agitprop was everywhere. Plans were completed and victories in the building of socialism won: a chorus of triumphalist reporting swamped documentary photography. The unchanged aspects of life were passed over in silence.

But the documents that have survived will not be silent, any more than the pages of history, or the lives destroyed in Stalin's time, will be wiped out. Astonishingly preserved photographs are surfacing from nowhere, and taking their rightful place in memory and history. ❏

Davlat Khudonazarov is a Tajik filmmaker. His documentary film Birth on the turnabout in the history and mentality of Tajiks in the 1920s, *relies heavily on the work of V Medved. All the photographs were found by the author in the Russian State Archive of photography and cinema.*
Translated by Irena Maryniak

OLIVIER ROY

The ties that bind

Islam is pressed into the service of the state as a bulwark against radical islamic forces from abroad

Islam has always been a central element in the identity of the peoples of the former Soviet Republics of Central Asia. In the Soviet era, the term 'muslim' was commonly used to distinguish locals from 'Russians' – more accurately, from Russian speakers since it referred equally to Jews as well as Christian Orthodox Slavs. As a result, Islam became an important stake in the battle between those competing for political legitimacy in the newly independent republics.

In the Soviet era, there were two quite distinct Islamic players: an official hierarchy and a parallel or unofficial clergy. The former was put in place by Stalin in 1943 as part of his four spiritual directorates or *muftiyya*. Few, and carefully controlled by the authorities, these clerics nevertheless developed significantly during the 1980s as Moscow sent younger mullahs to study in other Muslim countries. Many came under the influence of the Muslim Brothers: for instance, Qazi Turajanzade, head of the official clergy in Tajikistan, studied in Amman, Jordan in 1988; also Mohammed Yussuf, since 1989 spiritual head of the prestigious *muftiyya* of Tashkent and the supreme religious authority throughout Central Asia.

Even though all the mosques had been closed, an unofficial – or 'parallel' – clergy continued to work in the countryside throughout the Soviet period. The role was handed down from father to son and ensured the continuity of religious observances as well as the administration of important ceremonies such as circumcision, marriage and burial. Local officials turned a blind eye.

Contacts with the outside world were difficult and precarious throughout the Brezhnev era. While the unofficial clergy in the countryside was a conservative force, it was, paradoxically, the official clergy, as a result of their training in the Arab world, who introduced the notion of reform. This took the form either of 'modernising' religious practices or a return to a strict, fundamentalist version of Islam.

Militant Islam made its appearance in the 1980s. Intellectuals educated in the secular system were drawn to its militant and ideological character. Among these were Valiahmed Sadour, a Tatar from Moscow, and Abdullah Saïdov, a Tajik geodesic engineer. Today, under the name of Mullah Nouri, he is the leader of the Tajik opposition. But the militant Islamists never achieved the mass following and influence of their counterparts in the Middle East. In 1990, they founded the Islamic Renaissance Party (IRP), ironically the last 'Soviet' party of the union: they opposed independence from the Soviet Union on the grounds that it would divide the empire's Muslim population.

Perestroika, followed by independence, thrust Islam abruptly onto the public and political stage: mosques were built, religious tracts and literature were distributed; the unofficial clergy quietly took repossession of their old mosques; preachers, often from abroad, travelled the land. Islam entered the political lists and rapidly became something worth playing for. In the winter of 1991, the IRP split along ethnic, national and regional lines. Except in Tajikistan and Uzbekistan, where it challenged the new regimes that had emerged from the Communist Party, the IRP failed to establish itself firmly. In Tajikistan, it allied itself to the old Soviet *mufti*, Qazi Turajanzade, as well as to the nationalists and democrats, in an effort to dislodge the regime in power. Civil war erupted in 1992; by 1997, the coalition had been defeated and a fragile truce was declared.

The Islamist threat was rapidly sidelined in all the new republics: civil war in Tajikistan, the arrest of the PRI leaders in Uzbekistan – Abdullah Utaïev in 1992 and Sheikh Abdul Vali in 1995 – the banning of the party in Turkmenistan. In Kazakstan and Kyrgyzstan, where Islamisation was more superficial, the Islamists never succeeded in implanting themselves in any depth. They were swiftly contained and their rivalries confined to isolated pockets in places like the upper Garm valley in Tajikistan or Fergana in Uzbekistan.

However, the new governments were careful to fight Islam in the name of robust secularism modelled on that of Kemalism in Turkey. At the same time as opposing the Islamists, they needed to bring Islam the religion under their control and to make use of its symbols and images. From 1991, each republic established its own *muftiyya*, using the official Soviet clergy. In Uzbekistan, Kyrgyzstan and Tajikistan, it was not long before the muftis found themselves in opposition to their presidents: the muftis had reckoned on organising the clergy for their own ends, not those of the new states. Thanks in large part to funds from Saudi Arabia and the World Muslim League, they sought to establish a large measure of autonomy, including the establishment of their own training institutions. Faced with the task of bringing the official *muftiyya* to heel, the regimes bypassed the reformists and secularists, turning instead to the traditionalists and conservatives among the old unofficial clergy.

Bit by bit, the reformist muftis from the official clergy were removed: Turajanzade in Tajikistan went at the end of 1992, Mohammed Yussuf in Uzbekistan in 1993, Kamalov in Kyrgyzstan in 1995. The only ones left in position were the muftis of Kazakstan and Turkmenistan who happened to be on good terms with their incumbent presidents. Everywhere, 'Committees for Religious Affairs', government bodies, shadowed the *muftiyya* and ensured the clergy toed the official line. The new *muftiyya* had a monopoly on higher religious education: *mullahs* in small, unregistered mosques were not allowed to preach and had to be content with supervising prayers. The Turkish *Dyanet* – the Directorate for Religious Affairs, appointed by the prime minister – frequently supplied schools and scholarships for training the new government clergy as part of the bilateral cooperation between Turkey and the Central Asian republics. Uzbekistan was the only state to turn down Turkey's offers in this sphere. An *imam-khateb* appointed by the Committee for Religious Affairs had charge of all the large mosques, even where these were private foundations. In general, the authorities dealt with religious matters by carving them up into various administrative units: a *mufti* at the head of the state, an *imam-khatep* for each province, followed by one for each district or large town. Small mosques in towns and villages were left to their own devices as long as they left politics well alone.

Governments used the old unofficial clergy to secure control of Islam and bring the former reforming *muftis* into line. In this process, Qazi Turajanzade was replaced by an uneducated *mullah* related to the important traditional religious families connected with the religious (sufi) orders like the Naqshbandi, the Sharifzade and the Nematzade. The new *mufti* of Tashkent, Hajji Mukhtar Abdullah, was one such. All this was possible because, with minor exceptions, such as in southern Tajikistan or Fergana, the old unofficial clergy had never formed their own religious or political movements. Closely allied with local worthies such as the heads of *kholkoz* – state farms – they were, on the whole, apolitical and conservative. This made them far better allies of the new, conservative regimes than the reformists.

At the same time, governments were anxious to control the influx of visiting preachers and money from abroad. From 1993, strict visa regulations were effective in keeping Islamic preachers out of Uzbekistan. With the exception of small centres of local resistance, such as Fergana, the control of official Islam and the major mosques was everywhere assured.

Yet the states of the region, even where they remained firmly secular – though the word itself, *dünyavi,* does not always appear in their constitutions – were keen to lay claim to the symbolic trappings of Islam. Muslim festivals such as *id-el-fitr* and *qorban* replaced the old Soviet holidays like May Day and 9 May; all the presidents made the pilgrimage to Mecca; all their states joined the Islamic Conference Organisation. The Islamic past took precedence over the Russian era: the Syrian philosopher Al Farabi appeared on Kazak banknotes. At Bokhara in Uzbekistan, the mausoleum of Bahauddin Naqshband, the founder of the Naqshbandi order, was restored with Turkish money and the blessing of the state.

In many ways, it is often difficult to distinguish between the promotion of a past closely tied to Islam and the neo-conservative values that characterised the new states, particularly when it is a matter of traditional customs and practices. Women especially lost out with independence. Uzbekistan, for instance, passed a law on the *mahalla* – women's quarters – which legalised the social control exercised over women by family 'elders' who also often played the role of informal *mullahs.*

Another aspect of this 'Islamisation' was the promotion of an authentic, 'national' Islam as opposed to that which was 'foreign', 'imported' and 'unorthodox'. The former was represented by the Naqshbandi and Yasawi orders in Uzbekistan; the latter by Saudi Wahabism, the fundamentalism of the Afghan Taliban or Shiism. An authentic, national and moderate Islam was proposed as a bulwark against radical ideologies imported from abroad.

There is a good deal in common in the way the republics of Central Asia and the Middle East both use and control Islam. As in Egypt and Morocco, the state allies itself with the traditional clergy the better to fight radical Islam. The former are given a total monopoly over the training of new *mullahs* - though always under the supervision of the state. But there is one significant difference: nowhere in Central Asia – at least not yet – does Islam figure in the states' constitutional or legal systems. In none of them is Islam the state or even official religion; Sunday remains the 'holy' day and no element of the *sharia* has entered into official legal codes, not even into family law. In practice, however, while the increasing conservatism of these societies is drawing them closer to countries in the Middle East, at the end of the day, it is the Turkish model of control and containment of Islam that currently prevails in Central Asia. ❏

Olivier Roy *is director of research at the Centre National de Recherche Scientifique, France. His most recent book is* La nouvelle Asie centrale ou la fabrication des nations, *Le Seuil, Paris 1997*

ARKADIJ DUBNOV

Turkmen delights

The cult of the great leader is alive and thriving in Turkmenistan. There's not a lot of free expression, but with regularly paid pensions and salaries, free education and health-care, absence of inter-ethnic strife, a stable life in towns and villages and no crime, claims the President, no-one's very bothered

'The *Turkmenbashi* cult presents no threat at all to the outside world, you must understand that,' a well-placed member of the Turkmen leadership told me in private. It was sincerely said; it may even be true.

Turkmenistan is a little smaller than France with a population of just 4.5 million. The sands of the Karakum desert cover 80 per cent of its territory. The country is distinguished by the 'harmonious' combination of an eastern feudal tradition with a 'state' mentality formed over the past seven decades.

In the Soviet years, few people outside the borders of Turkmenia had much sense of what this far-flung republic might be like. What did Russian schoolchildren, for instance, know of Middle Asia (it became 'Central Asia' once more only after the collapse of the USSR)? They may have known that Tashkent was 'grain city', and that it had given refuge to huge numbers of evacuees from the European part of the Soviet Union during World War II. They knew about the steppes of Kazakhstan which 'nourished their vast country with corn', and about a lake called Issyk Kul somewhere in the Kyrgyz mountains (home of Chingiz Aitmatov, 'that great Kyrgyz Soviet writer' read, of course, by 'the whole world'). At best, they knew that Turkmenia contained the southernmost point of the Soviet Union, the town of Kuksha. Perhaps some also remembered that terrible earthquake in Ashkhabad in 1948.

That would be all.

Saparmurat Niyazov, who became First Secretary of the Communist Party in 1985, at the age of 45, created no illusions about the position to which his republic was relegated by the Soviet leadership in Moscow: the empire's appendage, its 'raw material'. With sovereignty as his legacy once the USSR had been dissolved, Niyazov, official historians write today, 'advanced a unique state model answering to the needs of a specific nation in a specific time in history'.

According to current official Turkmen historiography, the name 'Turkmen' first appeared at least 1,000 years ago. Their state emerged in the mid-eleventh century as a result of the creation of the Seljuk empire, and was subsequently lost in the second half of the twelfth century after Genghis Khan's invasion. After that the Turkmen lived 'divided under neighbouring feudal tyrannies'; it was almost seven centuries before, thanks to Soviet power, they regained their former territories.

Niyazov, who in 1991 proved himself to be one of the longest-surviving communist rulers of Central Asia, followed the traditional feudal recipe for preserving his position: he declared himself founder of the new Turkmen state and 'the father of all the Turkmen', *Turkmenbashi*. The procedures seemed legitimate in the Turkmen context: a gathering of the elders, *aksakaly*, and a recommendation of the parliament, the *majlis*, to publish the appropriate legislation.

'Turkmenistan is the creation of *Turkmenbashi*,' announces the sign with which the capital, Ashkhabad, greets its visitors. The logo of every newspaper is accompanied by the citizen's oath in one of three languages – Turkmen, English and Russian:

> '*Turkmenistan, beloved fatherland, country of my birth,*
> *I am with you ever, in my thoughts and in my heart,*
> *For the slightest wrong to thee, may my arm wither,*
> *For the slightest disloyalty to thee, may my tongue freeze,*
> *At the hour I betray my homeland, my president, your sacred flag,*
> *May my breath cease.*'

No newspaper, not even a sports paper, can appear without a photograph of the Great *Sirdar* (leader/chief) on the front page. No press independent of the state exists. There is no need for censorship since the papers carry no information which might be subject to it. The first page (all papers are just four pages) is devoted to official announcements; the second and third are filled with rubrics such as: 'Villagers' needs';

'School of management'; 'The spiritual world of man'; 'What lies behind the President's resolution'. The final page has advertisements and TV progammes. Finding out about events outside the country, either in neighbouring countries, the Commonwealth of Independent States (CIS) or Europe, is impossible. The outside world exists only insofar as it extends greeting to the 'Great *Sirdar*'.

Turkmen customs officials submit visitors' luggage to careful scrutiny. Russian-language newspapers are confiscated. Subscriptions to the Russian press are accepted for just a few days each year, and are severely limited by the tiny list of publications available. The cost of Russian papers makes them inaccessible to most. Although, surprisingly enough, it is possible to pick up Russian television's Channel 1 and see the news. Turkmen TV-time is taken up mostly by socio–political documentaries demonstrating the love of the people for their leader. They are simply constructed on the whole: street scenes and interviews, with portraits of the Great *Sirdar* in the background and monotonous music. A report on the President's visit to one of the regions will last two to three hours and be repeated several times over, in full.

Consider the following: the theological faculty of the Turkmen State University, built by the Turks, is to be opened with full ceremony in the presence of the Turkish Prime Minister Mesut Yilmaz and President *Turkmenbashi*. Hundreds of students bearing little flags cool their heels in freezing temperatures. So do we. A small group of girls can endure it no more, they slip off in search of warmth. A teacher is instantly on their tail and brings them back, like fugitives, angrily threatening every punishment in the book. At long last the Turkmen president and the Turkish Prime minister appear. The command is given: 'Shout!' Discordantly but noisily, with a kind of desperation, the students intone: '*Khalk, Vatan, Turkmenbashi*!' People, Homeland, *Turkmenbashi*!', the most frequently heard slogan in towns and villages throughout the country. Their faces show only relief that their torment is nearly over and that, soon, they will be allowed to go home.

Behind the students in the faculty courtyard stands a monument, three metres high, to Saparmurat-*Hajji*. (After a pilgrimage to Muslim shrines in Saudi Arabia a few years ago, the President added *Hajji* to his long list of titles). There he stands, eyes humbly downcast, holding out a mantle cast loosely over his shoulder.

Niyazov himself seems sincerely convinced that his personality cult is the shortest route to the formation of a 'state consciousness' for the Turkmen. The logic is simple: 'The greatness of *Turkmenbashi* lies in that he created Turkmenistan. For this the whole world respects the Great *Sirdar*, the symbol of the sovereign Turkmen state, while in his image, as in a mirror, the Turkmen venerate their statehood and take pride in their participation in it.'

Asked by the Russian paper *Trud* on 13 January 1997 about 'presidential portraits, monuments and busts round every corner', the Turkmen leader rallied. 'You mean, is it a personality cult? We are a traditional eastern society that has a profound – maybe at times too much so – fascination with its leader. But the personality cult is a communist phenomenon. If you think that regularly paid pensions and salaries, free education and health-care, absence of inter-ethnic strife, a stable life in towns and villages and no crime are signs of a 'cult', then by all means call it that.'

Dozens of streets, businesses, populated areas, even mosques have been named after *Turkmenbashi*: the former city of Krasnovodsk on the Caspian, the bay, the city's Freedom Square and the nearby village Jange, the jean production plant near Ashkhabad, the capital's airport, its main street and the mosque of the historical fortress Geok-tepe.

The richness and variety of *Turkmenbashi* iconography is bound to impress a visitor. That smile, so kind, so wise, adorns every state enterprise (there are no others) whether ministry, library or restaurant. The president's portrait also hangs over the Vatan cinema in the centre of the capital where prostitutes meet up for the disco in search of clients.

But all this strikes only the visitor. Local people have stopped noticing, just as they've stopped paying attention to the image of the Great *Sirdar* on the Turkmen *monat*, the country's currency.

About three years ago, Saparmurat *Turkmenbashi* let slip in public that he had US$3 billion in a Western bank account, either in Deutsche Bank or in Swiss banks, no-one knows exactly. People talk about it as though it were the most natural thing in the world. Clearly, the money comes from the country's natural gas exports. *Turkmenbashi* argues that someone has to answer personally for the protection of these resources and that people trust him. Last year, a Kazak paper wrote that the fortune of the Turkmen leader had almost doubled, and quoted a sum. In Ashkhabad everyone waited for stormy denials. There were none.

It is useless to try to understand how the country's budget is structured. Today Ashkhabad's exterior gives the impression that it is going through an investment and construction boom similar to Moscow's. Fashionable offices, hotels, hostels even, are being built everywhere. A trip down the capital's magnificent highway towards Berzengi takes you past five-star hotels on either side of the road, rented embassies, a vast (and empty) National Park and a huge National Museum built with Turkey's help.

Official statistics alone indicate that, with the participation of Turkish firms, 109 buildings are being put up for a total of US$1.8 billion including foreign investment of a little over US$200 million. Many of these buildings will house light industry, the rest mostly prestigious hotels and offices. Add the grandiose Court of *Turkmenbashi* built last year by a French construction company, with its gold bas-relief and waterfalls along the entire facade, officially estimated at S$120 million, and you can confidently say that treasury resources entrusted by the people to their president are not being thrown to the winds.

On 12 December 1995, the UN General Assembly accepted a resolution on the 'permanent neutrality of Turkmenistan. This provided another excuse for erecting monuments in Ashkhabad; amendments to the country's constitution for its oldest newspaper *Turkmenskaya iskra* to be renamed *Neitralny Turkmenistan*. The President became its 'founding father' (as he is of all the other main newspapers in the republic) and above its logo every issue proclaims: 'The first neutral state in the world recognised by the UN is our fatherland, Turkmenistan'. In honour of this historic event, an Arch of Neutrality, 62 meters high, is now being erected in the Turkmen capital. It will be crowned by a figure of *Turkmenbashi* 12 metres high. The monument is scheduled to be completed by Autumn 1998, for the seventh anniversary of the country's independence. Given demands by the IMF that unprofitable construction be suspended, this is widely thought to be unlikely.

Ordinary Ashkhabadians are unmoved, and only a little irritated by the Great *Sirdar*'s munificence. They are used to it. 'The Turks are doing most of the work, that's the trouble. It's not our people, not Turkmen,' they say. The construction ministry of Turkmenistan has ceased to exist; its role is being successfully performed by Turkish companies that employ their own people. Salaries received by Turkish workers and builders are 30 times those of Turkmen, who receive on average about US$30 a month. In some Turkmen ministries the post of deputy minister has been officially given to Turkish citizens who have taken on dual citizenship for the purpose.

Iranians are viewed with considerably more sympathy on a daily level, perhaps because Iranian business is less high-handed: 'We have always been neighbours,' members of the Turkmen intelligentsia say, 'and historically our borders were pretty conditional.' But only the Turks call the country 'the land of our forefathers' and feel no less comfortable here than at home.

There is little sign now of the Russophobia which marked life here in the first years after independence, when a Russian customer dissatisfied with his bag of tomatoes could be rudely dispatched with. 'Better go back to Russia, then. You're bound to find better ones there!' The Turkmen have found that what divides them from Russians – the carnage wrought by General Skobelev's army at Geok-tepe in January 1981, for instance – is less important than what they have in common.

The Turkmen President has been paying special attention to inter-tribal, as well as international relations recently, and his concern has been known to take on extravagant forms. On 19 May 1997, during celebrations in honour of that classic figure of Turkmen literature, the seventeenth-century poet Makhtumkuli, *Turkmenbashi* suggested additions to his widely known poems 'Weeping' and 'Turkmen state', where the names of Turkmen tribes are listed as Teke, Emud, Geoklen, Yazyr, Alili'. According to the Turkmen President, the names of three other tribes should be added: Ersar, Saryk and Salyr.

Five days later, on 24 May, *Neitraly Turkmenistan* published a statement from 15 poets, writers and academics under the heading, 'United in serving the Fatherland', proposing a re-issue of Makhtumkuli's poems. The authors supported the President's proposal that future editions should appear in a corrected form, and expressed the hope that the additions 'would not inspire any misunderstanding among readers'.

Which is how *Turkmenbashi* enriched the history of world censorship by providing the precedent for a blue pencil which augments rather than truncates, and for a 'positive' kind of censorship. ❑

Arkadij Dubnov *is a journalist and editor with Radio Liberty in Moscow*
Translated by Irena Maryniak

ORAL ATANIYAZOVA

Sea of troubles

The devastating pollution of the Aral Sea was the worst
environmental disaster to come to light with the collapse of the
Soviet Union. Its impact on the population of Uzbekistan is
worse than that of the fallout from Chernobyl, says a local
doctor, but no-one is doing anything about it

The environmental problem here is a dozen times worse than the consequences of Chernobyl, comparable to the situation in Vietnam where chemical weapons were used. The main problem is a result of durable and large-scale poisoning of the territory with pesticides and other toxic chemicals. There is also a shortage of water for drinking and agricultural purposes. Every year we have less and less water. This is the result of Kirgyz and Tajik industries in the upper stream of the Amudarya and Syrdarya rivers in Pamir and Tian-Shan Mountains – where there is also enormous pollution – discharging untreated waste into the rivers.

Credit: Rex/SPA

Agricultural chemicals and industrial wastes have been settling on the Aral Sea bed and in the deltas of the rivers for the last 40 years. Now it's like a gutter or sewerage pit. The dried bed of the Aral Sea has turned into a 'chemical' desert covered with a huge amount of toxic chemicals, especially chlorine-based pesticides. The dust and sands contain pesticides. As you know, pesticides don't disappear from soil and don't disintegrate for many years. Furthermore, in summer, pesticides are more dangerous because of the high temperatures. These toxic sands are blown over the territory; satellite research has indicated that they have even reached as far as Turkey and other European countries.

The most fearful effect of this is the cancer rate. Cancers, of the throat, liver, stomach, and leukaemia are growing rapidly. Women in Karakalpakstan have strongly marked disorders of the blood, immune and endocrine systems. This has a significant effect on reproduction and causes pregnancy and birth complications in 90–95 per cent of the women of this region. In the north of Karakalpakstan, where the environmental situation is at its worst, these indicators are even higher. The anaemia rate in Karakalpakstan is the highest in the world. Practically 100 per cent of our women and children suffer from anaemia. Even in Africa the rate is lower than here. I'm not speaking about the psychoneuropathic effect of the toxins in our environment. After the USSR collapsed, research into these questions was stopped.

There is a great deal of talk about the Aral Sea problem but nothing concrete is being done for the people living in this region. The World Bank, UN and WHO started their work in Karakalpakstan some years ago, but there are still no programmes aimed at improving the population's health or environmental protection. Nor have they set up any environmental monitoring programmes.

A great deal of money is being spent by international organizations, but the effect is minimal. Nobody wants to recognise the connection between bad health and environmental conditions. I read the World Bank's report saying that the level of minerals in the water is pretty high, but that the water quality is not dangerous. They state that the content of pesticides, heavy metals and other pollutants was not tested, yet claim that the situation is quite satisfactory and conclude there is no connection between the health situation and the environmental conditions. They ascribe the bad health in the region to poor culture and hygiene. This is more acceptable to them since it allows them to apply programmes used in the developing world with illiterate populations. One of the Soviet achievements here was a high literacy rate and very good hygiene. When internationl experts tell us that to improve our health we must wash our hands, most people just laugh at them. Most international projects don't use local specialists and apply experience from foreign countries.

People here have lived in this extreme situation for three generations. For them, this environmental situation has become almost normal. Indeed, 90 per cent of the people don't even understand that it's a problem. People get used to anything. For example,

Credit: Magnum/Susan Meiselas

when we ask a woman: 'What's your haemoglobin rate?' she says 'Oh, it's normal: 80g/l.' But a 'normal' rate should be 140g/l. In other words, people are getting used to the fact that to be sick is 'normal', to drink bad water is 'normal', to have poor nutrition is 'normal'.

People who have the acute form of anaemia acquire taste disorders. They like eating stones, clothes, synthetic materials. I met two kids of two- to three-years-old. In one year they had eaten about 20 kilos of

cloth. Their mother tells me that as soon as they had teeth they began to eat cloth. Every night she left them in the bedroom and in the morning she found them without pyjamas and sheets. They eat everything: carpets, blankets etc. They are like termites. They are victims of the Aral Sea crisis.

This illustrates the degeneration of our nation – human degeneration and qualitative changes in human behaviour. The women's and children's mortality rate in Karakalpakstan is the highest in the newly Independent States of the former Soviet Union.

If things do not improve this nation has no future. Speaking as a doctor and a scientist, I am very pessimistic. This is a severe test of our ability to survive. New hospitals and clinics are being built in Fergana, Navoi, Khorezm and other regions of Uzbekistan but not in Karakalpakstan. I see no hope of improvement if the current policy of the international organizations does not change. In 10 years I expect there to be a progressive growth of mortality and morbidity, a decrease in life expectancy.

Uzbekistan does not recognize Karakalpakstan as a zone of environmental disaster and is not developing any national programme to improve the health of the population or the environment. ❏

*Oral Ataniyazova is a Karakalpak obstetrician and researcher active in environmental and public health issues. In 1992 she founded the Perzent (Child) Centre to provide environmental education, medical services, publications and environmental monitoring. She was interviewed by **Anthony Richter**.*

KARAKALPAKS *are semi-nomads who trace their origins back to tribes living on the southern shore of the Aral Sea from the seventh century before the Christian era. By the sixteenth century they formed a multi-tribal nation occupying the territory between three kingdoms: Uzbeks, Turkmens and Kazahks. In 1873-75 the Karakalpaks joined the Russian Empire. After the Revolution, Karakalpakstan became part of the USSR. It was successively part of Kazakhstan and then of Uzbekistan. Today it is a 'sovereign' republic, with its own constitution, parliament and ruler, within Uzbekistan. The official language is Karakalpak; and there is a national flag, anthem and coat of arms. Politically and economically, however, the republic is dependent on orders from Tashkent, the Uzbek capital. Karakalpakstan occupies 30 per cent of Uzbekistan.*

JOHN MACLEOD

Media mirage

The President makes promises and the world turns a blind eye as he continues to silence the press and lock up the opposition

The media in Central Asia have made varied progress since the five republics gained their independence in 1991. Two countries, Kazakhstan and the Kyrgyz Republic, followed Russia in allowing considerable liberalisation, especially of the press. Although both the Kazakh and Kyrgyz governments have carried out some retrograde steps, including use of the law to muzzle critical journalists, the media are still relatively free to express a plurality of opinions. Most important, the Kazakh and Kyrgyz media remain free of the organised state censorship which stifles all free expression in Uzbekistan and Turkmenistan. The fifth republic, Tajikistan, is a special case: it is only now emerging from five years of civil conflict which left the media in tatters and many journalists dead or in exile.

Uzbekistan is located at the very centre of Central Asia and has the largest population; its development over the next few years will undoubtedly influence its neighbours, if only because they mistrust its regional ambitions. Under the grip of President Islam Karimov, Uzbekistan has made scant progress on either political or economic reform since independence. The media, too, have been kept firmly under control through Soviet-style intrusive censorship. Journalists are required to be slavishly loyal to the government line and risk dismissal or worse if they rebel. The resulting offerings in the newspapers and on radio and television are among the dullest in Central Asia. This is all the more sad because Uzbekistan was the region's academic centre in Soviet times and has a rich literary history going back centuries. It thus had the potential to be the leader rather than the laggard in fostering expression of ideas. The Karimov administration's record on repression of press

freedom is outdone only by the neo–Stalinist totalitarian regime in
Turkmenistan.

Journalism in Uzbekistan is not an enviable profession. No political
debate is allowed; nor may an alternative viewpoint on a non-political
subject of importance be expressed. Even economic data are off limits
because they are regarded as a state secrets. Journalists are reprimanded
for mild *faux pas*, and dismissed for open attempts at independence.

In January 1997, a new weekly paper, *Hurriyat*, went into print amid
rumours that it was to be allowed a small measure of freedom.
Amazingly, the newspaper did carry some critical material – deriding
state-run television for its appalling content, for example. *Hurriyat*'s
editor, Karim Bahriev, even held out against mounting pressure to
submit to having articles scrutinised by the state censor prior to
publication. In the end, however, the pressure was too great and by the
time *Hurriyat*'s sixth issue came out, Bahriev had been forced out and the
new editor, Khurshid Dustmuhammedov, was imposing censorship.
Bahriev was the third editor of a national paper or journal to lose his job
for publishing 'controversial' material in the space of a year. (Human
Rights Watch/Helsinki: *Violations of Media Freedom. Journalism and
Censorship in Uzbekistan*, New York, 1997).

The cowed media are only part of a broader picture of abuses of
human rights carried out by the Uzbek leadership in the post-Soviet
period. By 1993, the main opposition parties had been driven
underground, their newspapers banned and their leaders forced into
exile. The authorities went on to target other potential focal points for
discontent, singling out Muslim clerics and their followers who refused
to bow to the state-run version of Islam (See Olivier Roy, p130).
Dozens were jailed on trumped up charges; some are still incarcerated
nearly six years after they were arrested. Since November 1997, there has
been a wave of mass detentions of Muslims in the Fergana Valley, a
region the government watches especially closely for signs of unrest.

The government knows that unlike its rough treatment of the secular
opposition parties, the persecution of Muslim activists will not attract
loud complaints from the West. Perhaps it need not be concerned at all:
Western countries and international organisations have generally turned
a blind eye to human rights abuses in Uzbekistan, electing instead to
swallow the Uzbek government's line that it really is addressing its
slightly dented image, and that legislation recently passed on human

rights and the media will be put into practice.

The reality is that for now, at least, these laws are for foreign consumption only: human rights abuses continue unabated and the media is still heavily censored despite the legal prohibition of all forms of censorship. The United Nations, for instance, has uncritically poured thousands of dollars into the Uzbek government's new human rights institutions, which do little except whitewash the administration's egregious record. And international organisations based in Tashkent appear content to attend and even, on occasion, to finance government-staged seminars at which no discussion of the real problem is allowed.

Speaker after speaker stands up at these media meetings to praise President Karimov for his wisdom in ordering the media to be free, and chiding journalists for their slowness in taking up the offer. But there is never a word about continuing government control of the media, or about how every article in every national daily and weekly has to be seen and approved by the State Control Inspectorate before it can go into print. The SCI is the censorship office for the national press. It embodies the bizarre parallel realities of Uzbekistan in that it carries out an activity formally banned in the Constitution and media legislation, but does so openly and on the government's instructions. ❏

John Macleod *worked for* HRW/Helsinki *in Central Asia. He is now with the Economist Intelligence Unit, London.*

ZAMIRA SYDYKOVA

A small matter of corruption

The euphoria that characterised the early years of independence in Kyrgyzstan soon gave way to a more repressive climate in which a newspaper became the scapegoat for the wrongdoing of government

As the economy deteriorated, the nominally democratic government of the Kyrghyz Republic increasingly obstructed a press it saw as irresponsible and aggressive. The problem chiefly lay in the halting pace of economic reform and the absence of a welfare safety net for most of the population – and the growing evidence of corruption in the new regime. Credits from international banks in support of its reforms, and foreign investment, provided loopholes for state officials to siphon off funds for their own ends. It was something journalists could not ignore.

1997 was a difficult year for the staff of *Res Publica,* a newspaper covering social and political issues, founded with the dawn of democracy in Kyrgyzstan. It is financially independent of the government and has never represented any particular political interests. The editorial team and I, as chief editor, faced allegations of libel from Dastan Sarygulov, president of the state company Kyrgyzzoloto (Kyrgyzgold), and head of one of the most powerful branches of the economy, the gold-mining industry. We were accused of publishing a series of articles in which the paper attacked the fall in gold-output resulting from the suspension of work in a number of important gold-mines. The short-sighted policies of the head of Kyrgyzzoloto had failed to attract foreign investment throughout his time in the job.

The allegations presented against us by the city procurator were legally incompetent and overtly targeted our profession. We were told that data on gold-mining was a state secret; no arguments were produced to support Sarygulov's case that, as head of the industry, he had made any contribution to it. On 25 May 1997, I was condemned to 18 months' imprisonment by the Pervomaisky Court in Bishkek. Another member of the editorial team, A Alyanchikov, was sentenced to one year in a penal colony. Though this was not the first time there had been attempts to curtail democratic freedoms through the courts, public reaction was unprecedented. People demonstrated in Parliament Square, women with new-born children went on hunger strike. (I have two children myself.)

The wave of protest from international democratic institutions reached President Askar Akayev. For two and a half months I was tormented by law enforcement agencies. They shunted me from one colony to another. But on 5 August, after examining my appeal, the Kyrgyz Supreme Court yielded. We were both acquitted. The court acknowledged that the paper had not impugned Sarygulov's personal honour and dignity: there was no case for libel. In any case, according to the laws of our country, offences against personal honour and dignity should be tried under civil, not criminal, law.

Meanwhile, another employee of *Res Publica*, Yrysbek Omurzakov, also found himself behind bars. He too was hounded under the libel clause, and committed to prison before any decision had been taken by the court. Omurzakov had collected material based on comments made by the inhabitants of a hostel for factory workers and their families, who were being evicted because their employer had been declared bankrupt. A law on the privatisation of homes for those who had worked at the factory until then had already been passed. The outrageous behaviour of the liquidators contributed directly to the collapse of Kyrgyzstan's image as an island of democracy in Central Asia.

Yrysbek Omurzakov was amnestied by the President soon after our release. If only because the authorities in Kyrgyzstan have been given a lesson on how not to treat their journalists, we would like to think this kind of abuse won't happen again. No-one is prepared to give up the democratic privileges they have won. The public, as is its prerogative, has become the watchdog of justice. ❏

Zamira Sydykova *is the editor of* Res Publica

ROZA AITMATOVA

Wise women of Kyrgyzstan

It's the women of Kyrgyzstan who are shouldering the responsibility for leading the country out of a social and economic crisis

In 1916, shortly before the revolution, a rebellion in Kyrgyzstan against tsarist Russia was harshly suppressed. The Kyrgyz lost about 50 per cent of their population: it was genocide. Many people escaped to China. When the Soviet authorities took over, we were in bad shape. Soviet propaganda – 'land for the peasants'; 'power to the people' – made easy headway: people believed it. Our parents served the Soviet Union with genuine devotion.

Despite the negative side of the coin, Soviet power gave women a great deal. It not only created a female elite working under the aegis of the Communist Party, women in general found themselves in a far better position than before. Their status changed. They now participated in government, at least in the formal sense. The Soviet authorities paid serious attention to women's education and, on paper, to equality. When Soviet power stepped out of the picture, Kyrgyz women were in an excellent position. Over 97 per cent were literate; everyone had a secondary education; 60 per cent of adult women had a higher education. Women with large families were given substantial support. The children of shepherds living in harsh climatic conditions were taught in boarding schools.

Today, the public mood, and people's understanding of what 'democracy' means, seems to suggest that anything goes. The crime rate has shot up; privatisation has been carried out unfairly. Former party people have called themselves democrats and taken everything. Many people have been left penniless. The position of women has seriously deteriorated. Society has been polarised into rich and poor.

As factories and collective farms – *kolkhoz* and *sovkhoz* – fell apart, unemployment reared its head and women were the first to suffer. Suddenly, everything changed. Women looking for a way out of the situation went into suitcase trading. Now a woman will travel regularly to Ekaterinburg in Russia with cheap products which she sells at a profit. In the summer there are about 10,000 Kyrgyz in Ekaterinburg or Novosibirsk, Irkutsk, Omsk, Tomsk, Surgut; 80 per cent of them are women. They go away for six months to a year while the family stays at home.

The men are also unemployed; they can't support the children. They start drinking and the women sink under the burden. I know of two who died recently. How can a woman who can't afford to feed her children, or educate them, participate in politics? Economic issues must be resolved in parallel with political ones.

We have lost a lot – morally, educationally and economically. We want to be able to step out into the courtyard safely in the evenings. There are beggars in the streets – they were never there before; children who aren't at school, drugs, alcohol. And the victims seem to get younger and younger. People don't trust one another or the future any more.

The Kyrgyz were a nomadic people, but even then a woman had a voice in public life. She made peace when there were quarrels, people listened to her. Kyrgyz women never wore veils, because they had to move with their men and the cattle, and look after the children. A woman was responsible for preparing her *yurta* (tent) for transporting from place to place.

Let me tell you a story:

> Long ago there lived a *batyr*, Byurge-*batyr* he was called, and he had a daughter called Akshcherbet. She grew up very wise; she wrote songs and poetry, and played the *komuza*. At the time, Kyrgyzia was broken up into several khanates; one of the khans was called Kubat-bj. He was the ruler of a southern land. There was a quarrel between Kubat and Byurge and, later, to make up, they decided to marry their children. Kubat's son wasn't worthy of

Akshcherbet and she rejected him. Maybe he wasn't as clever. But they set about persuading her. 'If you don't marry him,' they said, 'our families will go on fighting and many will die. Can't you make this sacrifice for your people?' And she said, 'I can,' and married him. It is said that at their wedding she sang, 'Though he may not be wise, yet will I seek to make him so; though he may not be brave, yet will I make him so.' She married that there should be peace.

By and by, her father died and she came from the south for his burial. There is a custom that during funerals Kyrgyz women sit and weep and express their feelings through song. At this time two tribes – Solto and Sarbagysh – were at war in a northern land. Their representatives came to the funeral, and in her song she begged them to make peace in her father's memory. They considered, and asked her to sing again. And she did, and broke up the enmity that was between them and prevented the war which was about to begin.

Our women were traditionally wise and brave and persuasive – in ways that brought peace. That has remained: the drive to take responsibility at the critical moment. That is why they have become traders; that's why the Kyrgyz women's movement is so active. Women are trying to resolve things: they will do anything to rescue their children, families and community from the present crisis. ❏

Roza Aitmatova teaches physics at an institute of higher education in Bishkek.
Translated by Irena Maryniak

OINHOL BOBONAZAROVA

After the war is over...

After almost five years, the civil war in Tajikistan is nominally over but human rights continue to be abused daily. Chief among the offenders are the state law enforcement agencies

We used to have forced conscription here: people would be rounded up on the streets and then vanish. That's over now, but people are still disappearing, being punished outside the law and held without trial. Innocent people have been detained for up to three years. Last year 659 people are known to have disappeared. The mufti of Tajikistan was taken, his son and his brother. There's still no news of the son and the brother.

People were never taken hostage to this extent, even during the war. Even if you take the rebel movement, after the establishment of Soviet rule, these things didn't happen. It's new; it's not tradition. Just three days ago they found 10 corpses not far from the capital, Dushanbe. According to the Interior Minister, General Sharipov, 10,000 weapons are being illegally held by people at the moment. And it seems to me that official figures are always on the low side.

Incompetent people are being employed by law enforcement agencies: some have criminal records. They don't recognise authority. There was a feud recently between the former chair of the customs committee, Yakub Salimov, and General Suhrob Kasymov, the head of Tajikistan's inspectorate. It was war in the centre of Dushanbe. Many people died, including civilians.

Central power is weak and the regions are out on their own. There are strong opposition groups. Some people find the chaos to their advantage. They can take everything they want. Even President Rakhmonov admits that his orders are ignored.

Human rights can't be protected in these conditions. The killers of academician Asimov, who was killed last year, along with a number of other distinguished Tajiks, still haven't been found. He was the former president of the Academy of Sciences. The rector of the Medical University, Isaki, the director of the Institute of Medical Sciences, Professor Gulyamov and others were also killed. The authorities are unable to protect people's lives. War has undermined the centre. There are many informal leaders, 'heroes' of the time of transition, who are a law unto themselves. And there is the economic situation. The unemployed will carry out an assassination for just a few dollars.

Tajikistan's geographical position makes it vulnerable to the passage of drugs and arms: people buy them in Russia and other parts of the former Soviet Union. The Tajik problem has spilled over its borders. There's the Russian military contingent; and the increasingly active Iranian diplomatic presence. Peace in Tajikistan depends on Europe and countries in Asia: particularly on Russia, Iran, the UN, the Organisation for Security and Cooperation in Europe (OSCE) and other international bodies. Of course everyone has their geopolitical interests: Iran, Afghanistan, India, Pakistan, China, Uzbekistan, Russia.

The future depends very largely on Russia. The military forces here are mostly Russian. There are the Russian 201st division, the border guards and, since the peace agreement was signed in June 1997, Russian generals have been acting as consultants for the Tajik army. Russia wasn't neutral in this war. I don't mean democratic Russia, but the military industrial complex, the generals, the 'party of war'. When the peace agreement was made, Russia and Iran did a lot to move the peace agreement forward. The fact that leaders of the Tajik opposition were based in Iran seems to me to confirm that Iran has an influence and will continue to do so.

Between 1992 and 1994, the authorities of Tajikistan and Iran weren't on the best of terms. But Russia's geopolitical interests have changed: it is now closer to Iran. And the Tajik Republic's relations with Russia are very good. It brings Russia, Iran and Tajikistan closer. No one can dictate policy: Tajikistan is a sovereign state. But our economy is dependent, and there's the Russian army defending the country's borders – all that's bound to play a part. And Iran is us: the culture and traditions are the same. The Tajik intelligentsia supports cultural exchange and increasing cultural proximity, although they are wary of the Iranian regime.

We aren't any longer in a state of full-scale war. The last refugees have returned from Afghanistan. There was an exchange of prisoners and an amnesty. People were expecting a lot from the return of the opposition. The liberals who emigrated have almost all returned now. But many are unemployed and no-one listens to what they have to say. And there seems to be a power struggle within the opposition and the government which is disturbing the peace process.

Tajikistan has reached a crossroads. It could become a totalitarian communist regime (just holding a referendum would ensure that), or a 'democracy' along the lines of Kyrgyzstan, or an Islamic state. So far there have been only surface changes. Human rights were being abused before the return of the opposition and they are being abused today. Hostages are being taken on both sides. ❑

Oinhol Bobonazarova *is head of the Tajik Information and Analysis Centre for Human Rights and human rights advisor to the OSCE mission in Tajikistan* Translated by Irena Maryniak

MARK WEIL & ALEXANDER DJUMAEV

Shadow play

A theatre director and a musicologist in Tashkent talk about post-Soviet Uzbek culture and come to the gloomy conclusion that the past is repeating itself. The new government is exercising as tight a grip on artistic expression as its predecessors and woe betide those who step out of line

HOW ARE THE ARTS IN UZBEKISTAN FARING SINCE INDEPENDENCE?

Mark Weil: Living in Tashkent I cannot presume to speak about the whole of Uzbekistan. Tashkent is an argumentative city, always very conscious of being the fourth-largest city of an immense empire. It had a substantial intelligentsia, a fair degree of freedom, and a tradition of answering back – at least covertly.

Sadly, almost six years after independence, I don't have that sense of an intellectual viewpoint nearly so powerfully. The intelligentsia is split. One part of it has abandoned Uzbekistan altogether. Only a small part, perhaps, but the intelligentsia itself is not all that large, and the loss of even a small part is painful. When the authorities here produce 'feel-good' statistics designed to show that emigration from the republic has not been too significant, I always feel its not the quantity but the quality of those who have quit Uzbekistan that really counts.

I have a sense that Tashkent is becoming provincial. It has broken loose from the empire: it is enclosed now within its own boundaries and the city is rather taking it easy. The intelligentsia gets on with its life and its art. I'm often in artists' studios, and I see people still hard at work painting and achieving remarkable results.

I know rather less about literature. I have an uneasy feeling that

Russian-language literature in Uzbekistan is on the verge of extinction. I don't think Uzbek writers themselves have much idea of what is going on, and they seem to be publishing very little.

The theatre is more my territory, and there I see what Alim Salimov is doing in the Uzbek Theatre for the Young. But heaven forbid that he should stray into anything even remotely politically off-limits. He put on his own version of the life of Tamburlaine (Timur) in the Khamza Theatre, and it was banned immediately. I am not aware that there was anything particularly controversial about it, but it had only to depart in the tiniest particular from the current official idolisation of Amir Timur for the play to be doomed.

The intelligentsia has the choice of either endorsing official policy or keeping quiet.

UZBEK HISTORY IS BEING REWRITTEN. THINGS ARE BEING DONE THAT ARE HURTFUL TO LOCAL RUSSIANS, LIKE CONSIGNING TO OBLIVION THE NAMES OF MEMBERS OF THE RUSSIAN INTELLIGENTSIA WHO DID A GREAT DEAL FOR THIS COUNTRY AND ITS PEOPLE. STREETS ARE BEING RENAMED...

The Bolsheviks also tried to rewrite history. It's a tradition with us, an obsession. Each new regime tries to obliterate its predecessors. I would leave all the monuments of the Soviet era alone, only adding a plaque giving the date they were put up. It's all history. I really don't think it is very clever to erect a monument to Amir Timur in the centre of Tashkent. It verges on farce. No fewer than six monuments have come and gone there in the last 100 years; how many more replacements will there be in the future?

Who is it anyway who feels so negative toward Russian culture? Individual Uzbeks? 'The people?' Our audiences? No. Attitudes have not changed. Do the inhabitants of Uzbekistan now watch less Russian-language television or listen to fewer Russian-language radio broadcasts? If there was a survey showing that Russian broadcasts were no longer of interest, the politicians could quite rightly refuse to go on supporting them. I think there are some sharp businessmen behind this controversy. Since the Moscow channels are in such demand, they argue, why not make people pay to receive them?

The same logic is at work in other areas. On Victory Day a newspaper printed a photograph in which all the medals had been blanked out. Did they think Uzbeks who went through fire and water in World War II defending the Soviet Union would forget they had won Soviet medals? They want to manipulate our memory again as they did in communist times; that is no longer possible.

★ ★ ★

IS THERE A PLACE IN UZBEKISTAN FOR CULTURE WHICH IS NEITHER COMMERCIALLY NOR POLITICALLY ORIENTATED?

Alexander Djumaev: State subsidies for culture will continue in Uzbekistan for a long time yet . This is not only a Soviet tradition but a continuation of an Islamic tradition of patronage of the arts. Accordingly, the pressures on culture will continue. Although only about 1 per cent of the state budget is spent on culture now – in the Soviet period it could be as much as 3 per cent – additional resources are allocated for major official cultural enterprises, celebrations, anniversaries, etc. A celebration of the jubilee of Amir Timur included the making of a feature film and many books and articles on him. There is also an opera about Timur.

THE AUTHORITIES SEEM CLEARLY TO HAVE EMBARKED ON THE 'UZBEKIFICATION' OF CULTURE AND THE SUBORDINATION OF ART TO THE INTERESTS OF THE STATE WITH NO POSSIBILITY OF DEVIATION FROM THE OFFICIAL LINE?

The canonisiation of Timur does seem to be official policy; deviations from this are not welcome. Just as the figure of Lenin was sacrosanct in another time.

WHAT ARE THE PROSPECTS FOR RUSSIAN CULTURE IN UZBEKISTAN?

It has to be admitted that many members of the Russian intelligentsia in Uzbekistan are currently very depressed. There are many reasons for this, including material difficulties and the wretched wages paid in state cultural institutions. I know this affects even major figures among the Russian intelligentsia. They simply need to survive. Others see no future because they are constantly colliding with hostility, open or concealed, from cultural bureaucrats zealously enforcing their own line in the regions. Many have emigrated, others are planning to do so.

People who previously presided over Soviet Party ideology in its prime have risen to leadership positions in cultural policy. These people are now equally zealous in bringing down anything which does not correspond to their understanding of the new ideology.

DURING THE SOVIET PERIOD, ESPECIALLY AFTER THE DEATH OF STALIN, A MAJOR PART OF CENSORSHIP WAS SELF-CENSORSHIP. DOES THAT CONTINUE?

Anyone who survived the Soviet period still has that inner censor sitting in them to some degree, that master-slave mentality. They are constantly anxious about the possible consequences of their actions and lives, living in an all pervasive state of apprehension. The bureaucrats are expert at exploiting this: as in the old days they manipulate information, and conceal it when necessary. ❏

Mark Weil is a theatre director working in Tashkent. He was interviewed by Yury Yegorov for the September 1997 issue of Literaturnaya Gazeta. Alexander Djumaev is an independent scholar and musicologist living in Tashkent. He was interviewed by Anthony Richter and David Rieffe. Both interviews translated by Arch Tait

**MUBORAK SHARIPOVA &
SHAHRBANOU TADJBAKHSH**

Babel: Widows of Tajikistan

*T*he human toll of the Tajik civil war is not yet fully known. In the short
period of fighting between the summer of 1992 and the spring of 1993, up
to 50,000 may have died and 500,000 fled to neighbouring Afghanistan or
became internally displaced. One undisputed factor is the war's heavy toll on the
lives of women. In just one war-torn southern region, more than 20,000
households are now headed by women. Many lost their husbands to war, others to
the crime that is now endemic in Tajikistan.

Tajikistan is a patriarchal society in which women living without men are
accorded little respect. When they marry, Tajik women marry into their husband's
families, moving in to live with the in-laws. The death of their husbands makes
them, in a sense, internally displaced persons.
Shahrbanou Tadjbakhsh

SHODIGUL MIRZOEVA was born in 1967 in Hissor. Before he
disappeared, her husband worked at the Central Department Store.
During the war, he looked after many relatives who fled to his house:

'One day, at 8:00am, he got up and measured the feet of all the
kids. He wanted to bring them shoes, and his sisters warm clothes,
and he went to work. According to witnesses, he had been at
work only two hours and then gone to the village of Choriakoron
to collect the clothes. He went into the store and, as he came out,
some gunmen from Hissor met him at the door and took him
away. They confiscated his car and threw him into an
underground chamber. He survived for three days, then sent a

letter to his father to pay a ransom for him. The letter arrived too late; in any case, the relatives didn't have enough money.

'His neighbours found the underground passage, but did not find him. At first, we hoped his friends from Hissor would have saved him, but after a few days, rumours that he had been killed started. I only found out two years later that he had been shot in the face and chest. His sisters found people who recognized him from his pictures and said they had dug his grave themselves.

'At the time they killed my husband, I was pregnant with my fifth daughter. My other children were very small. I stayed home for three years after this incident. My neighbours and my three brothers helped, as did my relatives. This war left has left me with five kids at the age of 25. The 2,000 Tajik *sums* (cUS$4) pension that I get, after running around for it for so long, gets me nowhere. I received some humanitarian aid last year, which was much needed. Last year I went to the village and rented a few metres of land and worked on it for four months. From this I got two bags of onions, one bag of potato and one of wheat. I don't know what will happen to me. I don't know how my children will study. You need money for books and pens, which I don't have. Once in a while my neighbours help me. That is how I am surviving.'

★ ★ ★

ZULFIA NURMAHMADOVA was born in 1966 in Shaartuz. She has four children, three sons and one daughter. During the war she became a refugee in Afghanistan. Her husband was killed on 13 November 1992:

'We were living in Shaartuz, where the Uzbeks used to live. When the war broke out I took the kids and fled to my mother's house in Kumsangir. My husband and our male relatives all stayed behind: they said they were innocent, they didn't need to become refugees. Then we heard that they had put him, two of his brothers and two of his nephews, one 15 and the other 18, into an ambulance and killed them. I know it was our own neighbours who did it. Later we found the bodies and buried them. My mother in law, who had raised five sons without a husband, became ill from grief and died six months later. His eldest son became a refugee in Afghanistan, and hasn't returned yet. I came back from Afghanistan with another one of her sons. Our house was completely destroyed, our stuff stolen. I have been slowly putting my life together again, rebuilding the house. My brother in law is helping me. We are selling what we have left, that is how we are living.'

★ ★ ★

MUKARRAM SA'DULLOEVA was born in 1963 in Dushanbe.

'When I was 17, I married Khokim Rashidov. He was born in 1955. He was an orphan like me. He had studied in Riga and worked at Prison No 1 in the town. We met at a wedding and fell in love, then we married in Kofernihon. After the wedding, we continued to live in Kofernihon, with his mother, who had five children. We lived for three and a half years in that house. But space was very tight, and his work place gave my husband a dormitory. In 1989, we bought a house.

'We had four children then, now I have five. Thank God they are all healthy, but now they are all orphans. On 7 February 1994, my husband gave a ride in his own car to the prison workers and didn't return himself. In the morning we went to his work place. They said last night he had taken someone home. Everyone started looking for him. After a week they found his body in the hills outside the city. He had no holes in his body but was all black and blue. They must have beaten him and tortured him. We buried him that day. The local mosque had announced that they had found a body, and the head of our neighborhood identified him.

'In the first year, we received some help from the Red Cross. We got rice, macaroni and clothing every three months. Before I had never worked. After the death of my husband I started selling bread. I make about 2,000 Tajik rubles (US$4) a day, and I get another 2,000 a month as pension for my kids. I go to stand in line to buy bread at 5.00am, then I stand in the street and sell it until 8.00 or 9.00pm, rain or snow. I sell about 100 pieces before lunch, and about 50 to 60 after.

'My eldest finished his school with excellent grades. He

dreamed of enrolling in the university, but I couldn't make enough money. He now works in a bakery from 6.00am to 7.00pm. My second one left school when he was eight. His intestines were hurting. The other two don't study either. My 12-year-old daughter does all the housework.

'I have no hope of anyone's help. Thank God we are alive I say to myself everyday. What else can I do?'

★ ★ ★

GUZAR SAKAEVA was born in 1956 in Kuibushev. She has never been to school.

'My father died when I was three years old. My mother, who was a gynaecologist, went to Komsomolobid, married again and had more children. She has eight kids now. In 1973, she married me off to Ne'mat Tolibov. At first, we lived in Kofernihon and my husband was a truck driver. When we had more kids my husband went to Qurghon Teppa to make more money. He bought a house and we had some things of our own.

'But during the war they burned everything and we became refugees back in Kofernihon. My husband went back to his work as a driver, this time driving long-distance buses. We had seven kids then. My husband used to take me on his trips, perhaps he was scared to go alone. The last time it was around the time I was due to give birth. Nevertheless he asked me to accompany him on a trip. I didn't feel right about this trip at all. At that time I was at my mother's house with the kids. It was like he had some kind of premonition or something, because he took us from my mother's house and said goodbye to his mother in law. We all came home and he said, "Get ready, I will go to Faizobod to get some gas for the car and to see a couple of friends. Then I'll come back and we'll make the trip."

'I bathed and prepared some food for the road and waited for him. After lunch they brought his body to the house. I was so shocked I fainted. My kids were wailing around me. They said it was an "accident".

'After the death of my husband I went to his mother's house in Komsomolobod, but there again there were problems. After a while I brought back some of my kids to Dushanbe and started begging, door to door. I gave away my eldest daughter to a man, without a legal marriage or anything. A policeman was killed in our neighbourhood and they blamed it on the local kids, including my 20-year-old son. When they came looking for him, he flew to Russia, and I haven't had any news from him in four years. He didn't even know that his father has died. Now I live in some teacher's house. I don't have a house. I make these patties from bread and onion and sell them in the bazaar for 50 sum each. That is how I am making a living. My kids don't go to school. I also work in people's houses. And the teacher is threatening to kick me out every day.'

★ ★ ★

ANORGUL BERDIEVA was born in 1965 in Kofernihon. She has two children. She lives by selling bread, out of which she makes 700–800 Tajik *sums* (US$1.50) a day on average. Her husband, Zulfikor Davvaev, was killed in 1994. Before his death gunmen had threatened him many times.

'I used to live very well with my husband. He had a good salary, we had two kids, we had our own house, we lived there with my in-laws. One day he disappeared. His body was found by the river after three days. They said he'd died of head injuries.

'I lived with my parents for a while, but that couldn't go on, so I rented an apartment with a friend and started working in the bazaar. I pay 4,000 *sums* (US$8) a month. I found myself the apartment. There is no-one to help, certainly not the government. My mother is looking after my two kids. I go to see them on Saturday and Sundays. If I work well I make 1,000 sums a day. But what kind of money is that, nothing. You can buy just 10 pieces of bread with it. This is how I am living.

'Before, when I had a husband, it was good. He used to take care of all my needs. What man will now do the same? What man will help me out now? These men of today, they just want to have a good time. My husband's relatives don't help either. When he was alive, his parents helped us a bit. Afterwards, they said: "My son is dead, get up, get up and leave. What can I say. He was my kid. Now he's dead, and you're not my kid." My mother-in-law said this to my face. She said: "Come on, get up and leave." They said: "What are you staying here for? You are young, you should marry again or not, we don't care any more. Just go."

'My whole concern is housing now. My brother helps me a bit. I tell myself, maybe I should go and live in Russia. Maybe there I'll get a house. I hear of Tajik women, working in kitchens in Russia, cooking, washing dishes. I am thinking of the future of my daughters. The eldest one must go to school this year. One school uniform costs 25,000 *sums* (US$50). I don't know what to do: pay for the house, feed my children, or help my parents. If I had any sons, it might have been different. My husband's family say if I had had a son, I might have a home now. They say girls belong to other people, they're no good."' ❑

Muborak Sharipova is a Tajik psychologist and founder of the NGO Free Asia, which supports the psychological rehabilitation of women victims of violence. She lived in exile in Moscow from 1992-1997 and recently returned to Dushanbe.
Translated and introduced by **Shahrbanou Tadjbakhsh**, a researcher who lived in Tajikistan while writing a PhD on women in that country.

AHMED RASHID

Pipe dreams

China's entry into the Great Game presents a challenge to other leading players. It threatens Russia's grip on its former republics and is a check on US ambitions in the region

During the past 12 months, China has evolved as a major player in the new 'Great Game' – the rush to acquire oil and gas reserves in energy-rich Central Asia and the Caspian region. China's strategy has been fuelled by the growing energy demands of its extraordinary economic growth at a time when its domestic oil production is stagnating and its over-use of coal creates an environmental nightmare. Paying up to twice the going rate, China is gobbling up foreign oil fields around the world, but especially in Kazakstan.

China is also dramatically expanding other links with all five of the Central Asian Republics. It has secured border treaties with Central Asian states that share a frontier with China, expanded trade and investment links and, in return, has demanded that neighbouring states do not support the growing threat posed by Uighur nationalists and Islamic fundamentalists who are trying to carve out an independent state in China's Xinjiang province.

Since May 1997, China has put down US$8.2 billion for oil concessions in Sudan, Venezuela, Iraq and Kazakstan. Add to this the cost of pipelines China is committed to building from Central Asia, and Beijing's total commitment comes to US$20. 7 billion.

China is the world's sixth-largest oil producer; but by 2020, while domestic oil production will have peaked at 200 mmt (million metric tonnes), demand will outstrip it by more than 200 mmt. China aims to fill the gap by rapid expansion abroad, particularly into Central Asia. Not only is Kazakstan adjacent to Xinjiang, allowing for oil pipelines directly into China, it is also a natural land bridge to Iran and Iraq where the Chinese envisage even greater future expansion. In June 1997, China National Petroleum Corporation (CNPC) purchased 60 per cent of the Aktyubinskmunai Production Association in western Kazakstan at a total cost of US$4.32 billion. The field's reserves are estimated at 140 mmt of oil. In August, CNPC purchased 60 per cent of the Uzen field at a total cost of US$1.3 billion. Uzen has estimated reserves of 200 mmt of oil.

China also needs to stabilise an increasingly unstable region. On its vast western borderland China faces the long-running bloody civil war in Afghanistan, a still simmering civil conflict in Tajikistan, and bloodshed in Kashmir – conflicts fuelled by Islamic fundamentalism, ethnic nationalism, weapons and drugs – a dangerous cocktail that makes China extremely nervous.

There is another conflict even closer to home. Beijing's immediate concern is to provide economic development and jobs for its own separatist-inclined, violence-prone and only Muslim majority province of Xinjiang. By developing close economic links with Central Asia, linking the region with pipelines and activating economic development in Xinjiang, China hopes to calm the Xinjiang region and its restive Uighur population (See p173).

The break-up of the former Soviet Union revitalised the aspirations of Chinese Uighur separatists and nationalists who are demanding a separate Uighur state. Islamic fundamentalism amongst the Uighurs has been fuelled by contacts, training and weapon supplies from Islamic radicals in Afghanistan and Pakistan. In 1997, China faced the worst violence, unrest and riots in Xinjiang since 1949.

China has also secured border agreements with all the Central Asian states. During a visit to Moscow by Chinese President Jiang Zemin on 24th April 1997, the presidents of China, Russia, Kazakstan, Kyrgyzstan and Tajikistan signed a treaty on improved border security and a comprehensive demarcation of borders which have been in dispute since the Russian Revolution. In return, China received commitments from Kazakstan and Kyrgyzstan that they would not give support to Uighur dissidents based in these states; some 200,000 Chinese Uighurs fled to these states after China occupied Xinjiang in 1949.

Trade between Xinjiang and Central Asia has grown from virtually zero in 1990 to US$775 million in 1996. This is apart from the lucrative cross-border smuggling trade, estimated to be well over US$1 billion. Kazakstan's imports from China rose from 4 per cent in 1990 to 44 per cent in 1996; total two-way Chinese-Kazak trade was US$460 million in 1996. More than 100 joint ventures have been set up between Chinese and Kazak entrepreneurs.

However, China's overall strategy in Central Asia will depend on the success it achieves in realizing the oil pipelines it plans to develop. These could well alter the geo-strategic picture in the region for both the rest of the world and China. China plans to build four major pipelines.

Russia wants an Asian market for its massive Kovyktinskoye oil and gas fields near Irkutsk in Siberia. But while it is keen to lock in China as a major market for Siberian gas, it is less keen to see China emerge as a major player in Central Asia and jeopardise Moscow's grip on what it still considers its own backyard. The US has no such objections to China's pipelines which they see as a stabilising force in the region. US oil companies, on the other hand, are troubled by competition from CNPC and it's willingness to pay excessively high prices to secure new oil concessions in Kazakstan and elsewhere in the region.

Kazakstan, meanwhile, is desperately keen for China to start construction of a planned US$3.5 billion oil pipeline from Uzen to Xinjiang. Kazakstan's dependence on foreign exchange earnings from energy exports to Europe via Russian pipelines would be reduced, a new market for Kazak oil in Asia would open up and, for the first time, the country's oil fields in the west would be connected to population centres in the east. For lack of a cross-country pipeline, Almaty currently receives its oil and gas from Siberia.

Along with Japanese and US companies, China is also pushing ahead with preparing a feasibility report for 'the pipeline of the century'. This would pump oil from Turkmenistan, Uzbekistan and Kazakstan to China's coastal regions and onwards to Japan – a US$22 billion project.

China has offered to build a strategic 1,000 kilometres pipeline costing US$2 billion from Uzen in Kazakstan across Turkmenistan and Iran to Bandar Abbas on the Persian Gulf. From there tankers could ship oil to China's coastal cities and westwards to Europe. In September 1997, China and Kazakstan signed an agreement to build the first 250 km spur of this line from Uzen to the Turkmenistan border. Such a link would put China in a favoured position for future energy supplies and, more important, offer Iran an opportunity to bypass US sanctions and become the main export avenue for Central Asian oil, giving it the strategic and regional clout it is looking for.

But there are serious US and Russian objections to giving any north–south pipeline that would give Iran such a strategic grip on Central Asian oil exports. Russia would also oppose any Chinese move that would free Central Asian oil and gas exports from Russian control. ❏

Ahmed Rashid *is a freelance journalist working in Pakistan. His book* The resurgence of Central Asia: Islam or nationalism *was published by Zed Books, London in 1994*

AZAT AKIMBEK

The making of a nationalist

Unlike Tibet, which has its spiritual and political leader in the Dalai Lama, the Uighurs have no political leadership to take their case to the world.

For China, Uighurstan is a vast source of raw materials. Just as the Soviet Union drew on the resources of Kazakhstan and other republics, so China sucks oil and gold from Uighurstan. It has deployed several Pakistani rockets on its nuclear base on Uighur land, at Lobnor.

China is unlikely to return the country to the Uighurs without serious resistance. If there are disturbances in Tibet, or someone has been arrested, the news is broadcast worldwide within 24 hours. The Dalai Lama has an impressive network; we don't. It was only thanks to US and European journalists that the world came to know about the Kuldzhe tragedy in February 1997. We live in an informational vacuum.

And there is the Islamic factor. We Uighurs are Sunnis; the Iranians are Shiites, so are the Chechens. The Shiites are orthodox, fanatical. Sunnism is softer and more tolerant. Islam is humility. These days the whole world talks about Islamic terrorism – even though I am convinced it was the Chinese who blew up two buses in Urumchi, and that the events in Kuldzhe were inspired by the special services in order to provoke the Uighur intelligentsia. It's time-honoured Chinese policy to despatch opposition leaders and show clemency to their supporters. It happens every two or three years. That's why we don't have a leadership. Our leaders are shot.

My father was condemned to death in 1953, when the repressions began under Mao Tse Tung. So was my grandfather; but they didn't shoot him because, as a prince, he carried immense authority. So they simply put up a poster: 'enemy of the people'. There you have him: the exploiter, the landowner. Judge him for yourselves. It's much what happened under Stalin.

Chinese soldiers marched him round for two days (he was already 89) encouraging Uighurs to spit on him and beat him. Not a single Uighur ventured to abuse or hit him: he had always been held in great respect. And the Chinese lost their nerve. They didn't touch my grandfather, but they ordered my father to be shot. My father was an officer, a captain in the national army. My mother, sister and I were advised to escape to the Soviet Union.

We risked our lives and reached Chuachak, on the border of the Semipalatinsk region. In 1954, Khrushchev invited the Kazakhs, who had gone to Xinjiang, back to the Soviet Union and my mother registered herself as a Kazak. That was how we got into the Soviet Union. We spent seven years without citizenship or a home. My grandmother had hidden one-and-a-half kilos of gold and jewels in a hollow walking stick, and we survived on that.

We did eventually acquire Soviet citizenship, and I went to Samarkand University. When they found I was a Uighur, they expelled me. It was the policy of the first secretary of the time, Rashidov. I didn't speak Uighur then. Now I speak it fluently. My mother had been first lady back home, she was trained as a lawyer. In the Soviet Union she washed floors in the filthiest TB dispensary for children in Kalinin. I'd pick her up in the evening and she'd be weeping. I was conscripted into the Soviet army. They abused me and called me a Chinese spy.

And then I began to ask myself – why is it that they keep humiliating us? It was only after the army, when I was 20, that I discovered who my grandfather was. And, very quietly, I became a Uighur. I'm 48 now and have been speaking Uighur fluently for about two years. In the Soviet Union they called me a Uighur nationalist because I wanted to speak about my history or culture. Anyone – German, Korean or Uighur – who took an interest in their own culture was branded a nationalist.

And so I thought: that's fine by me. Yet I still don't think of myself as a 'nationalist'; I'm just a Uighur who wants to talk about his history and culture. ❏

Credit: Ian Berry/Magnum

Azat Akimbek is chairman of the Lob Nor Anti Nuclear Committee. He also heads the Azat Akimbek Foundation, a non-governmental charitable organisation.
Translated by Irena Maryniak

ANTHONY RICHTER

To stay or not to stay, that is the question

Russians, many of whom have been in Central Asia for three generations, are faced with the difficult choice of taking the hard road home or staying on in countries where they are now a minority

When the USSR was dissolved on Christmas Day 1991, it set off a population movement of historic proportions, particularly from Soviet Central Asia. Without Moscow's control, the residency rules that kept many people artificially pinned down in Central Asia disappeared. Free to go, the peoples deported there by Stalin in the 1930s and 1940s left in large numbers. A million descendants of Catherine the Great's *gastarbeiters*, the Volga Germans, left for Germany, while hundreds of thousands of Crimean Tatars, Chechens and Meskhetian Turks also left for their historic homelands.

In 1989, Russians in Central Asian numbered 9.5 million, 20 per cent of the population. Already one fifth of these – more than 2 million people – have left. Actually their exodus began in the mid–1970s, when local population growth began to displace outsiders in education and other professions.

But Russian migration accelerated and changed after the fall of communism. Formerly, as representatives of the centre, the Russians occupied important positions out of proportion to their actual numbers. In Soviet times they dominated key bodies in the Communist Party and occupied critical positions throughout the former Soviet Union. But since the collapse, fear of ethnic conflict, economic hardship and worries about the future have changed the rules for Russians throughout Central Asia, shattering their previous sense of security.

Their changed situation is reflected by the proliferation of new terms to describe the Russians' new status. Observers from Moscow, like presidential adviser Emil Payin, have called them, colourfully, 'an imperial minority', or 'a new diaspora'. They are also referred to as 'compatriots', which has a nationalistic ring to it. Another term, both vague and maddening, is *Russkoyazychnye*, 'Russian speakers', which lumps together all Slavs and non-natives. Then there are the returnees to Russia, the 'forced migrants', refugees, or simply *repatrianty*, 'resettlers'.

The Russians had many motives for coming to Central Asia. Some, like colonists everywhere, came opportunistically to find easy jobs and good housing in a pleasant climate without needing to learn a foreign language. Others were simply 'allocated' there by the state like so much capital to be used in fulfilment of the 'Plan'. Then there were 'the exiles and escapists': gulag veterans who never left the region after prison, or the political and intellectual outsiders who sought to live in relative freedom far from the control of the Soviet metropolis. Nineteenth-century imperial Russians in Central Asia saw themselves as combining a civilising mission with the securing of commercial advantage in border trade or precluding the possibility of a British threat from the south.

After the revolution the Russian presence was recast in terms of Marxist-Leninist progress, friendship and internationalism. Large numbers of Russians provided administrators for the Communist Party and the skilled labour that industrialised Central Asia. In the 1920s, the first Five-Year Plan tripled the Russian population in the region. Further increases followed during World War II when hundreds of factories were evacuated to Central Asia, and in the postwar period when enthusiastic youths answered Khrushchev's call to 'plough the Virgin Lands of Kazakstan'.

The Central Asian Russians' disorientation today is linked to their nostalgic attachment to their former Soviet identity. More than others in the USSR, they thought of themselves as Soviet citizens in Almaty or Tashkent, USSR, rather than Russians in Kazakstan or Uzbekistan. Central Asia was a place of residence, and their homeland was the Soviet Union. When the Soviet Union disappeared and the Kazaks, Turkmen,

Kyrgyz, Uzbeks or Tajiks acquired new nationality in states that bore their name, the Russians were left feeling cut off from Moscow, abandoned on the archipelagos of their settlements in Asia, deprived of the context and ideas that justified their presence in the region.

Central Asia's Russians also see themselves as 'better Russians' than those who stayed home. By virtue of their patriotic homesteading experience and living in a more temperate and modest culture, they have become superior. They think they work harder, drink less, and are more successful. On returning to Russia, this attitude evokes a hostile reception in their new places of residence, particularly in small Russian villages. Central Asian Russians tell stories of returnees having their house burned down or being run out of town.

Within the Russian community, responses to the changes of the past few years have been contradictory. To nationalist, patriotic politicians like Georgy Tikhonov these are not just 'hard times' but a new 'Time of Troubles', a period of national calamity for the Russian nation, like the one it suffered in the early seventeenth century. Tikhonov, a communist who ran mammoth Soviet construction projects like Tajikistan's Nurek hydroelectric station, and now chairs the Russian Duma's Committee on the Commonwealth of Independent States (CIS) and Compatriot Affairs, claims that 'the crisis is not only in Central Asia, but also in Russia'.

Tikhonov's parliamentary committee was set up to protect the political, linguistic and cultural rights of Russians in the former republics. Because many of the new republics will not offer dual citizenship Tikhonov's committee has proposed the establishment of 'compatriot status'. This would protect Russians abroad, but the committee has not yet agreed on a meaning of 'compatriot'. If this fails, up to 31 December 2000, any citizen of the former Soviet Union may claim Russian citizenship. In 1995 the Russian Duma also established a formal Compatriots Council that brings together Russian parliamentarians with leaders of cultural and rights groups with names like Hope, Harmony, Friendship from every former Soviet republic. They convene regularly in Moscow, but it is not clear whether they are generating anything besides moral support. A Federal Migration Service headquartered in Moscow is supposed to deal with return of 'forced migrants', an ironic parallel to the Transmigration Authority the Russian Empire created in the last century to help volunteers colonise its periphery.

The Russian government's actions are themselves contradictory and create confusion among the Russian communities. Is the Russian Federation encouraging them to stay put or to return to Russia? Lidia Grafova, who runs a refugee rights group to aid *repatrianty*, points out that at first the message seemed to welcome return, but that this does not correspond to the reality. Grafova believes that 'Russia's geopolitical interests now consist of keeping Russians in those places where they are being squeezed out'.

A new Russian policy draft asserts that 'policy towards compatriots

Dushanbe Tajikistan, 1996: Staying on is hard to do - Credit: Susan Meiselas/Magnum

abroad is aimed at their socio-political integration into the framework of new state structures and at restraining emigration to Russia.' Russians in Central Asia are sceptical of the rhetoric and policies of bureaucrats in Russia. One group of Russians in Tajikistan wrote: 'Russia, declaring its protection over Russians in the CIS, in practice is doing everything it can to bring us to the brink of death. Our numerous letters and appeals go unanswered and the answers we do get are heartless form letters.'

Back in Russia, Yabloko party member Vyacheslav Igrunov says that conservatives in the Compatriot Affairs Committee believe in the idea of resurrecting the Soviet Union and using the Russian communities as a fifth column. 'This idea is dead,' he maintains, 'since the policy has no basis in reality, and the Russian diaspora is not oriented in that direction.'

It is difficult to understand the implications of various local policies directed at Russians. While the latter sometimes allege discrimination on ethnic and linguistic grounds, their charges are often exaggerated. For example, their charge that the ascendance of local languages is a means of purging Russians from government jobs. Central Asian officials for their part have given repeated assurances that Russians' fears about the prospects of their linguistic, educational, cultural and professional rights are unfounded. The leaders of Uzbekistan, Kazakstan, and Kyrgyzstan say they wish the Russians would stay, but at the same time have not guaranteed dual citizenship nor that the Russian language will have full official status. Dr Aikanysh Abylgazieva, an adviser to Kyrgyzstan's President Akaev, confesses that the language debate in parliament remains unresolved and constitutes 'an undeclared policy, even though it isn't the policy of the President'.

The pace of Russian departure has stabilised for the moment. While many feel caught in an ambiguous situation, between the policies of Moscow and the nation-building policies of its former republics, the road back to Russia is hard and uncertain and their future in Central Asia insecure. Until their perceptions and circumstances change, they must make do in purgatory: as an ethnic minority, as 'Russian speakers', as compatriots or as *repatrianty*. ❑

Anthony Richter is a specialist in post-Soviet affairs.
Research for this file and the Caucasus file (Index 4/97) was made possible by a grant from the Netherlands Ministry of Foreign Affairs, and was carried out in collaboration with the Glasnost Defence Foundation and Dosé na Tsenzuru.

BARRY LOWE

Of Mongolia and mushrooms...

20December 1997

The border troops at Ulaanbaatar's small but modern airport, frost-rimmed in mid-winter, its misted windows looking out on a snow-bound tarmac, have the tallest peaked hats in the military world, matched in dignity by their long-skirted steel-blue greatcoats and their brightly polished boots. They are stern but friendly. The soldier who stamps my passport says, 'Welcome to Mongolia,' in a voice that lingers melodiously over every syllable. At the exit barrier is a familiar face, Sunji, one of the staff from the Press Institute of Mongolia where I'll be working for the next week. She's beaming at me from beneath a tall fox-fur hat.

The drive into town from the airport passes a hill crowned by a monument left by departing Russian soldiers at the end of their 70-year stay. It's a statue of appalling ugliness whose thrusting social-realist lines moulded in concrete serve as a reminder to Mongolians of what they have turned their backs on, and of their current efforts to build a modern market economy and democratic society out of the ruins of their socialist experiment.

The surrounding mountains are deeply carpeted with fresh snow. A frozen river winds across empty fields, children tobogganing on its tree-lined banks. White pencil lines of smoke rise from the *ger* towns, suburbs of white-walled Mongolian tents or *ger*, on the city's edge. Four factories dominate the skyline: the three electricity plants and the Ahki vodka factory, an important institution in this nation of spirit drinkers.

I'm on a mission to expose a small number of Mongolian journalists to some western ideas on ethical standards in journalism. Mongolia's press has taken on some decidedly tabloid characteristics in its recent, post-communist, evolution. It's a trend that is causing widespread concern in the country as newspapers increasingly emphasise entertainment over information and show less regard for accuracy or responsibility. The Press Institute of Mongolia, established to train Mongolian journalist in western approaches to media practice, has asked me to conduct training courses in ethics for working journalists and for trainee reporters. The Press Institute is a non-government organisation funded by foreign aid agencies, mainly the Danish aid agency Danida. Its director is Tsendiin Enkhbat, a committed, energetic former journalist with an engaging manner and a ready smile.

21 December

A day for strolling the wide streets of Ulaanbaatar. It's minus 15 Celsius, which the locals say is unseasonably warm. There hasn't been snow for days and the pavements are crusted with a black, iron-hard rind of treacherously slippery ice. At nine in the morning some all-night drinkers are still on erratic paths homeward. One is arguing violently with a young woman. He grabs her arm and almost flings her to the ground. She breaks away and flees as he hurls a torrent of abuse at her. Passers-by take little notice of the spectacle.

The goal of my outing is Sukhbaatar Square which, in size and grandeur, is up there with its better-known counterparts: Tiananmen in Beijing and Red Square in Moscow. A line of shivering photographers, standing behind rickety display boards exhibiting their work, try to entice customers from among the few people that wander across the vast empty space. The square is named after the leader of Mongolia's 1923 socialist revolution, whose enthusiasm for transforming Mongolian society into a Soviet-style Marxist state was not shared by the hundreds of thousands of people who died in his bloody purges.

22 December

Mongolians are not the world's greatest builders, which is hardly surprising in a country where the majority of people still live in tents. Take the staircase in the Mongolian Press Institute building: each stair is unique, with a different size and different slope from all the rest. For people used to uniform stairs it seems almost impossible at first to climb them without tripping. But after a few attempts you start to get the rhythm of the ascent: when to take a big step, when to lean forward, and so on. The staircase of the Institute building held terrors for me on my last visit. I have to relearn its eccentricities.

My first class comprises 15 newsmen and women, their ages ranging from 28 to 51. Most are print journalists. Nearly all the print journalists work for unashamedly tabloid publications that have names like *Alarm*, *Top Secret*, *The Truth* and *Oh, These Women*. These reporters have rich experiences to draw on for our discussions about situations where journalists have to make ethical decisions. *Top Secret's* representative, for example, recently got a scoop with a sizzling yarn about the captain of the Mongolian basketball team having an affair with Miss Mongolia while his wife was in hospital giving birth. Unfortunately for the journalist it turned out his dad was a close friend of the basketballer's dad and that his brother-in-law worked for the basketballer's dad's car-hire company. There were some unpleasant repercussions.

Its feet planted firmly in the mud, *Alarm* is the out-and-out market leader, boasting sales of 25,000, far more than the *Today*, the only quality independent. Also well-favoured is the police department's own newspaper *Vice and Virtue*; something of a misnomer since it rarely contains stories about virtue. Although Mongolia has a high literacy rate, the newspaper market, remains small, barely exceeding six figures. Some newspapers have to make do with a circulation of just a few hundred. Their TV counterparts do only marginally better. Apart from state-run Mongol TV, there are two independent stations: Eagle TV, which enjoys financial backing from a South Korean Christian group, and Channel 24, owned by the same group that published *Today*

Alarm's reporter was hot on the trail of an African tourist who had allegedly being spreading Aids among Mongolian women. Her front page story said the visitor from Cameroon had infected at least 25 virgins, aged between 13 and 18, who had queued up at his hotel door for a chance to have sex with the mysterious Romeo. The health department later gave a much less sensational version of the affair.

The more senior members of the group contributed anecdotes about media practices and restrictions in the old days. One had lost his job for writing a story - never published - about a drunken Russian truck driver who ploughed into a group of schoolchildren killing three of them and who was subsequently spirited out of the country without facing punishment.

23 December

I'm curious about the newspapers my class members write for, so I head out, after breakfast, to a Peace Avenue news-stand. There is a bewildering range of titles on display, at least 40 of them, spread over wooden benches like a monochrome quilt.

When Mongolians heard the word freedom seven years ago they reached for their printing presses. Independent newspapers have been sprouting like mushrooms since the 1990 democratic revolution: 550 at last count. But this explosion of news activity has left some problems in its wake, not the least of which is the quality of reporting and news-writing in a country still largely unaware of Western values in news production. In their haste to get into print, publishers have neglected the finer points of news production, creating a deluge of poorly reported, poorly written and poorly designed newspapers that many people believe are undermining the country's chances of building a mature and responsible media tradition.

24 December

I take advantage of a break between training sessions to catch up with a man I met on my last trip who could be described as the father of Mongolia's free press. Tsendiin Dashdondov is president of the Mongolian Free Democratic Journalists' Association, the organisation that spearheaded the campaign to unshackle the Mongolian press from government control at the time of the democratic revolt. He occupies a tiny office crowded with stacks of yellowing newspapers above a grim, windowless bar known as the Journalists' Club.

As we share cups of pungent tea, he rails against the poor standards and lack of professional ethics shown by Mongolian journalists today, accusing them of wasting their chance to create a socially enlightening press industry.

'After 1990 newspapers appeared like mushrooms after rain,' he tells me. 'But since then the image of the free press has been damaged by unqualified, untalented journalists publishing newspapers and periodicals of poor journalistic quality. A free press means one qualified to comment on government actions.

'At the moment the social and political situation in our country is extremely complicated. The public is unused to thinking and analysing for themselves. In these circumstances journalists need to publish reports based on hard facts rather than mere rumours or opinions. If we fail to do this we will not only fail to make our society more accountable, we will also give those who seek to control the press a reason for reintroducing censorship.'

25 December

I awake on Christmas morning to a new sound: it's a normal working day but the traffic outside seems strangely muted. I look out of my window on a city transformed by a heavy snow fall. The snow is still falling thickly, piling up against the shop fronts and frosting the heads and shoulders of pedestrians.

I feel it's a day for some form of spiritual activity and decide to pay a visit to the Gandam monastery, one of the few surviving relics of the days when Mongolia was a staunchly Buddhist nation. Before the communists came to power Mongolia rivalled Tibet as the centre of tantric Buddhism. At the turn of this century there were more than 700 monasteries dotted across the country and about a third of the male population were monks. But by the time the communists' anti-lamaist purge was over, only three monasteries remained standing and more than 30,000 monks were dead.

Today Mongolia is experiencing a religious revival and at each dawn in Ulaanbaatar people crowd the courtyards of monasteries queuing to enter halls where saffron-robed lamas sit in rows chanting *sutras*. In the Gandam monastery forecourt a line of old women, eyes streaming from the cold, prostrate themselves in the wet snow before a weather-worn *stupa*. Inside the main hall, crowded with gilded images of the Buddha, the yellow light from candles and the oily smoke from butter lamps suffuses the air with a warm glow. On a bench at the back of the room a young novice aged eight or nine is struggling to stay awake, his head drooping over the text he has to read. An old monk prods him gently each time his chin falls on his chest.

26 December

The great Hurral of the People, or the Mongolian parliament, exemplifies the architecture of fear. It sits massively and foreboding across one end of Sukhbaatar Square, a severe reminder, in unrelieved grey, of the remote and oppressive nature of the regime that constructed it. I am delivered to its portico by a black maria. Earlier in the week a local TV station – Channel 25 – had reported on my ethics training course in its evening news bulletin, interviewing me and some of the participants. The news item was seen by a senior member of the government, Dashzhamtsiin Battulga, who heads a standing parliamentary committee currently drafting a new media law for Mongolia. Mr. Battulga has summoned me for a chat. We meet in a committee room, sitting opposite each other at the centre of a rectangular table long enough for 40 people. Mr. Battulga explains that one of the chief tasks of his committee is to complete the transfer of state-owned media entities to the private sector. His committee is looking for foreign models of media regulation. It is concerned about the excesses shown by the new Mongolian press but is reluctant to intervene in any way that might suggest a return to the old days of state control. I talk to him about press councils, broadcast advisory bodies and Australia's anti-media monopoly laws.

I have a thick wad of *tugrigs* – the hyper-inflated Mongolian currency – lying unspent in my pocket. I suggest to my colleagues that I spend the money on a party, at my place, for the Press Institute staff. The idea is approved enthusiastically. By eight o'clock that evening my tiny sitting room is packed with large Mongolian bodies sprawled across every square foot of floor space. Mongolians tend to party in a unified way; there is one focus of activity, one conversation. Guests take turns in providing entertainment: one person will recite a poem, another will sing a mournful song.

It's the coldest night of the winter so far: minus 30 Celsius. Most of the guests leave at 11pm, their faces ruddy from vodka and talking. But a few of us are not ready to call it a night and we head out into the frost to sample Ulaanbaatar's bars. There are plenty to choose from. Among the trendier places is the Matisse Bar where entering involves running the gauntlet of an army of teenage beggars who prowl the car park wrapped in layers of rags and cast-off clothing. The city currently has a problem

with homeless children, victims of the economic hard times that have come with the transition from socialism to capitalism. They sleep in the entrance halls of apartment buildings and in the sewers and prey on the population's conscience.

We end up at Emon's bar where some Russian engineers are staggering drunkenly around the dance floor; a table of bored-looking prostitutes watch them with dwindling expectations. By the time we leave there's just enough time for breakfast before my car for the airport arrives. Enkhbat is there, bear-like in his sheep-skin and fur hat. He stuffs my bag with vodka bottles and tells me about the old trick of fooling customs agents by carrying vodka in plastic mineral water bottles. I'm not convinced it would work. ❏

Barry Lowe teaches journalism at the City University of Hong Kong

FRANK FISHER

The ratings game

Cyberspace may yet fall victim to the electronic blue pencil

Consider this 1996 comment from the Singapore Minister of Information and Arts: 'Censorship can no longer be 100 per cent effective, but even if it is only 20 per cent effective, we should still not stop censoring... We cannot screen every bit of information that comes down the information highway...'

In those far off days the Internet truly seemed anarchic and untameable. 'Information wants to be free' was the war cry, and Clinton's authoritarian Communications Decency Act was roundly reviled, despised, circumvented and finally despatched, shot down by the Supreme Court as unconstitutional. A thousand websites strobed in victory as their keyboard-punching architects struggled to find a direction for their world-conquering freedom. Yet, even then, the clouds of hysteria regrouped; the porn, the cruel and deliciously funny rumours

Rating, filtering and the PICSRules - the techie stuff

Filtering doesn't always require prior rating, and rating doesn't inevitably lead to filtering, but the two are increasingly intertwined and, often, erroneously equated.

Website rating in its simplest form can be likened to the certification of movies or computer games - site developers, or any third party, might decide that a particular page was judged suitable for over-fives, or over-18s. A web-user, or more often the parent of a web-user, might decide to preset their viewing software, their browser only to access sites of a certain rating level. Until recently, restricting Web access using ratings has been conducted mainly on an experimental level, as few websites contained a rating.

PICSRules

It seems now as if that limited truncation of the Web may be about to accelerate. In concerning our public figures, the dummies' guide to producing weapons-grade amphetamines from household chemicals (mothballs, always mothballs), the terrorists' homepages and the Drudge Report; what was to be done? Not where to draw a line, but how to maintain it? How could we keep our children on the straight_and_narrow.com?

Big Government had failed; it had woven the first links of the Web decades before, and it loved the commercial possibilities from the unexpected success the WWW had become, but even Clinton's media-savvy acolytes couldn't regain control, so they turned to the industry. Even as the CDA was receiving it's judicially applied last rites, Vice-President Al Gore was appealing to software developers: give parents the tools to filter the internet, let individual households draw their own line.

The libertarians and net activists drew a sigh of relief and went back to their coding, contented.

December 1997, the World Wide Web Consortium voted to accept a system of labelling, and put it forward as a standard for the entire web. The group of 200 scientists and software developers, generally known as W3C, chose a system known as PICS – Platform for Internet Content Selection – which will give anyone from schoolboy HTMLers to military dictatorships a powerful and extremely flexible ratings language. Rather than the simplistic '18s and over' certification of the past, PICS will enable the rating of sites according to many scales at once, and not just the traditional parameters of sex and violence. PICSRules allow for the construction of many ratings systems upon them. A concerned parent may want the flagging of violent pornography, an authoritarian government may require notification of opposing political views. All systems are possible with PICS.

Rating and filtering

That is only half the story: PICSRules, and the systems which use them, only *label*

Soon, however, the dreadful possibilities opened up by a full-blooded commercial drive towards on-request filtering became clear. For millions of Web users – those accessing through educational establishments, libraries, cyber cafés and the workplace – the choice of whether to filter or not was taken out of their hands. Software installed on desktop machines, or at the Internet service provider's net gateway, carried the preferences not of the user, but of the machine's owner or manager. For all those people with controlled access, the Web is shrinking, day by day.

It is rare now to find a library terminal that supports unfiltered access, indeed there are US proposals to deny federal funding to organisations, particularly libraries, that don't use a recognised filter software. Senator John McCain, an Arizona Republican, has just proposed a bill which would cut funding unless schools and libraries certify with the Federal Communications Commission that they will use a filtering device on computers with Internet access, so that students will not be able to access sexually explicit sites or other material deemed 'harmful'. The bill also has strong Democrat support.

The American Library Association takes the position that libraries should provide unrestricted access to information resources; it characterises the use of blocking programs as censorship. And what

content. It is the filtering systems that cut access to sites. Filters already in use do not, in the main, use PICS – the technology is too new. The methods currently employed by restrictive governments and internet providers to limit Web access on their side of the modem link, and by individuals and organisations to control browser access on *their* side, divide into two basic types, both of which involve software that takes note of a Web address or URL (Uniform Resource Locator) and checks a database to see if that URL is on a permitted list or not. It is how the URL gets onto that list that differentiates the two methods.

Some organisations attempt to rate manually every new Web page that appears, (estimated at 10,000 to 20,000 a day and rising), using teams of researchers. One manufacturer of domestic 'censorware', SurfWatch, employs freelancers with specialist knowledge of, among other things, bondage, hate speech and improvised munitions – which rather calls to mind the old anxiety of who guards the guards...

censorship these filters can provide! The Electronic Privacy Information Centre conducted an examination of one kind of filter – that used in conjunction with established search engines – and found that a trawl using Alta Vista's 'Family Search' and the full Alta Vista search engine for information on the NAACP (National Association for the Advancement of Coloured People) resulted in only 15 sites being passed as suitable by Family Search, compared with the 4,000 presented by Alta Vista. Ninety-nine per cent of sites were blocked. That level of censorship was repeated in searches for 'Unicef', 'Christianity', 'the Bill of Rights' and others. All told, more than 90 per cent of sites were unavailable to filter-bound users. In a Kafkaesque touch, the user is never aware of just how restricted his search is - there is no whiff of smoke to alert us to these burned books.

Desktop-based filter applications are similarly extreme in their censorship; Cyber Patrol blocks feminist and atheist discussion groups, HIV resource pages, the Animal Rights Resource Site and criticism of itself and other major players - the popular site 'Why America OnLine Sucks' is a taboo location for many of these filters.

the techie stuff

On the other hand, the majority of censoring organisations and governments use software agents to scan the web, searching for clues to a site's content. Being dumb strings of code, these agents merely look for what they are told to look for, generally words within a webpage's content or HTML structure which, individually or in combination, might be thought to flag a page's purpose. This automated censoring is known as 'pattern blocking'. Naturally not every Web developer is perverse in quite the way software companies such as NetNanny or CYBERsitter expect him to be; so many 'rogue' sites still get through.

Even so, both methods have been shown to over-filter substantially, and both automatically block any site that they cannot, for one reason or another, access.

It is when we speculate on the future for filtering software, running alongside a massive expansion in self-rating/third-party rating using PICSRules methods, that the impact upon free speech becomes apparent.

CYBERsitter is famed for its overzealous approach; one pagan found her site blocked not only for her use of the words 'wicca' and 'mistress', but also 'beer' and 'wine'. Spurred by the First Amendment, Jonathan Wallace, editor of *The Ethical Spectacle*, published an article entitled 'Purchase of Blocking Software by Public Libraries is Unconstitutional'. CYBERsitter blocked it.

Again, for the ordinary user there is no way of knowing just what sites are being blocked. Most software companies send out their update information in an encrypted form – your software can read the file and update its lists; you can't.

In addition to add-on filters, a new threat to free speech on the Web has arrived with Microsoft's latest browsers. Internet Explorer 4 is loaded as the default browser in the majority of new computers, and it comes with a PICS filter capability built in. IE4, together with the new breed of filter-friendly search engines, has the capacity to make Internet censorship seamless and all pervading. As a truly global player, Microsoft's decision goes a long way towards putting state-of-the-art censorware within the grasp of every censoring power on earth. Think of the Singaporean Minister mentioned earlier – whose browser do you think he'll want in public libraries?

Rather than the hit and miss of pattern blocking, or the expensive and time consuming manual search, censoring states, organisations, or individuals can develop their own ratings profiles and implement those profiles either on individual desktops or via internet service providers.

The results could drastically change the web: at one level commercial pressures from advertisers looking for maximum hits may lead many sites towards inoffensive, ratings-friendly content, in much the same way as broadcast TV has abandoned challenging programming in a quest for numbers – the bland leading the bland. At another, authoritarian governments are being handed a tool with which they can nullify criticism or dissent in an instant.

It is easy to imagine a system whereby a state granting internet access via proxy servers, proxy caching, and choke points (all methods of restricting access – inwards and outwards), might demand compliance with its own PICS-based ratings profile. Just as now, sites would probably be rated by the state concerned, or even by a commercial organisation, and only rated sites would be viewable. But there are two major differences further down the line, apart from the speed and simplicity of the PICS filters. First, Internet censorship has become a mainstream political goal- how can the

But this is apparently precisely what the US government hoped for. Vice-President Gore said, 'Our challenge is to make these blocking technologies and the accompanying rating systems as common as the computers themselves.'

Or as Marc Rotenberg of EPIC puts it, 'We are creating an architecture for blacklisting and censorship unparalleled in history.'

The World Wide Web hangs by a thread. ❏

Frank Fisher

Further information:

> *http://www.epic.org/Reports/filter-report.html*
> *http://www.gilc.org/*
> *http://peacefire.org/*
> *http://www.freenix.fr/netizen/213-e.html*

the techie stuff

West complain about abuses in the Far East when Microsoft is building PICS compatibility into its latest browser with Clinton and Gore's impassioned support? Second, the W3C group protocols are superbly effective. Previous rating systems of the kind used in Singapore and China had an obvious flaw: once the page had been rated, and its URL OK'd back at the Ministry of Truth, a cunning free speech enthusiast could simply change the content of the page without changing its title or URL, thus getting a different message across. At least until the next ratings check.

PICS provides for a rock-solid defence against such public-spirited chicanery – using strong encryption technology of precisely the kind that governments the world over are trying to keep from their people, PICS will allow a digitally encrypted signature to be placed within the ratings code. Not only will this act as an authenticating seal, it will also contain within it a 'checksum' result for the Web page, created by taking the entire page information, and running it through a specific algorithm. This checksum figure can be recalculated automatically when the page is requested and, if the page content has changed since it was rated and approved, the request will be denied and the rating withdrawn.

Prince Claus Award for Index

Jan Herman van Roijen and Hilde Jansen of the Royal Netherlands Embassy presenting the award to Index editor Ursula Owen.

We were honoured to be the recipient of a Prince Claus Award for 1997. The presentation took place on 19th of December at the Netherlands Embassy in London. The award was presented by the Ambassador to the United Kingdom, His Excellency Jan Herman van Roijen.

The Prince Claus Fund for Culture and Development was established to mark the seventieth birthday of HRH Prince Claus of the Netherlands on 6th of September 1996, for the purpose of 'expanding insight into cultures and promoting interaction between culture and development.'

'Since its inception Index has become the refuge for writers, journalists, scholars, human rights activists and students, recording violations of human dignity and fighting for an open global society. After 25 years of immeasurable achievement Index deserves to be awarded recognition and honour.'

Malawian poet Jack Mapanje

'Index is to be congratulated on its 25th anniversary. The Prince Claus Fund pays tribute to an initiative which opened up the way towards free, independent literary publishing, and to its courageous and longstanding activities on behalf of freedom of literary expression, especially in non-western countries.'

From the report of the Prince Claus fund Award committee 1997.